Chippen and the Wilts & Berks Canal

Chippenham Studies 2

Ray Alder

First published in the United Kingdom in 2011, on behalf of Chippenham Museum & Heritage Centre, by The Hobnob Press, PO Box 1838, East Knoyle, Salisbury SP3 6FA.
© Ray Alder 2011

British Library Cataloguing in Publication Data
A catalogue record for this book is available from the British Library.

ISBN 978-0-946418-89-3
Typeset in 11/13 pt Octavian. Typesetting and origination by John Chandler
Printed in Great Britain by CPI Antony Rowe Ltd, Chippenham

Acknowledgements

I would like to thank the following who have given me invaluable help in writing this book:
Chippenham Museum and Heritage Staff, Mel Barnett, Paul Connell , Jewels Shore and Julie Brind. and of course my fellow wardens who have all been so supportive.

The Wilts and Berks Canal Trust, far too many people to list, but a special thank you to Jan Flanagan, Peter Williams and Doug Small for their time and help researching this book. I would also like to thank the Trust for allowing me to reproduce pictures from their archive.

Similarly, I would like to acknowledge and thank the Kennet and Avon Canal Trust Archive, Wiltshire and Swindon Archive, Somersetshire Coal Canal Society, The Wiltshire Archaeological and Natural History Society and The Chippenham Gazette and Herald.

Thanks are also due to Mike Stone for his guidance and help in the editing of the book and John Chandler for his invaluable advice.

In addition, I am grateful to the many people who have kindly shared their memories and family histories with me; far too many to name individually but it is this unwritten history that brings the story of the canal to life.

Finally, I would like to thank Pete and Lou Canning for sharing the canal experience with me, but my biggest thank you goes to my family, Gil, Jonathan and Emily, for being there and supporting me. Thank you Jo for your photography and artwork.

Ray Alder
February 2011

Cover illustrations include: an artist's impression of Brinkworth's boat, by Jo Alder; John Trow on the *Faith* at Chippenham Wharf (see page 56); and details of canal art and signage.
Title page illustration: Detail of a door from a canal boat. Canal collection at Lackham College.

Foreword

This is the second in a series of Chippenham Studies books published by Chippenham Town Council, based on the work of the team of knowledgeable and enthusiastic volunteers at Chippenham Museum and Heritage Centre. The key aim of the museum service is to work with and to promote the heritage of Chippenham. *Chippenham and the Wilts and Berks Canal* written by Ray Alder is a magnificent addition to our understanding of the history of Chippenham. Chippenham Town Council is proud to support this series of books.

Sue Wilthew
Chief Executive,
Chippenham Town Council

The exceptional work of ongoing restoration and aim of returning the Wilts and Berks Canal to a navigable waterway by the volunteers of the Wilts and Berks Canal Trust has been well publicised. Indeed visitors to various stretches of the old canal can see the results of their efforts, with several sections in water today.

What is less well known is the history of the canal, and its importance in the development of the town of Chippenham. The canal, built in the years from 1795 to 1810, was cut from Semington near Melksham to Abingdon on the Thames. It linked with the Kennet and Avon Canal to form part of a nationwide network of waterways to transport coal, timber, stone, salt and agricultural produce.

The arm to Chippenham is largely forgotten or ignored today. If it is remembered it is as the local tip. Completed amid various litigations in 1801 this ran from the Wharf in Timber Street and joined the main Wilts and Berks Canal near Pewsham.

There is very little remaining; the Wharf is occupied by the bus station and the rest is under roads or engulfed by housing.

Ray Alder, a volunteer at Chippenham Museum and Heritage Centre has painstakingly examined original documents, photographs and records for information relating to these local canals. He has surveyed and walked the route looking for the remains of structures and has talked to local people who can still remember the canal in the town.

Ray describes the planning and building of the Wilts and Berks canal, its slow decline, decay and finally abandonment. He introduces the readers to the characters who lived and worked on the canal and lists his hopes for the future of the waterway.

The result is a scholarly and relevant book that will be enjoyed by all.

**Melissa Barnett
Curator,
Chippenham Museum and Heritage Centre**

Further Chippenham Studies to be published will be

3   *From Domesday to Demolition: A History of the Flour Mill in Chippenham, Wiltshire* 1086 – 1957 by Dr K.S. Taylor.

4   *The Story of Chippenham Carnival* 1923 – 2001 by Don Little

5   *Inns and Innkeepers of Chippenham* by Joan Blanchard

6   *Brunel, Brotherhood and Early Railway Engineering in Chippenham* by Mike Stone.

General Editors are Paul Connell and Mike Stone. Chippenham Museum & Heritage Centre would like to thank senior staff of Westinghouse Rail Systems Ltd for part funding this series from royalties earned from *A Hundred Years of Speed with Safety*, by O S Nock.

Further ideas for titles in the series should be submitted to the Editors via Chippenham Museum & Heritage Centre, 10 Market Place, Chippenham, Wiltshire SN15 3HF. Telephone No. 01249 705020

Contents

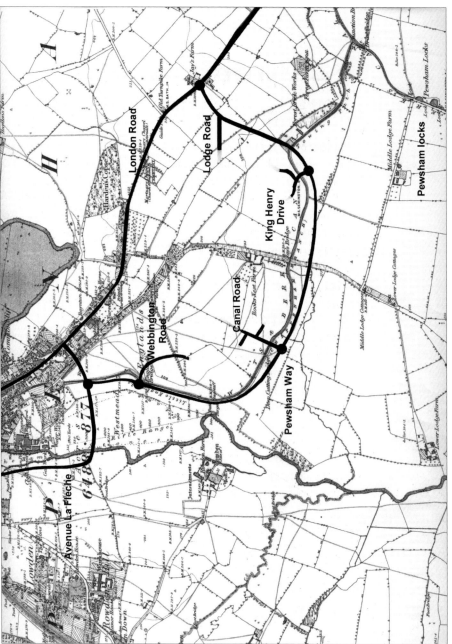

Ordnance Survey Map of 1889 showing the Chippenham branch of the Wilts and Berks Canal with today's roads superimposed.

1. Introduction to Chippenham's Canal

This book is about Chippenham and the Wilts & Berks Canal. It is not a history of the canal, rather the story of the canal in Chippenham and the surrounding villages of Lacock, Pewsham, Derry Hill and Stanley. It is the meeting point of town and canal and charts and reflects that history, sometimes turbulent, from the canal craze of the eighteenth century to the canal's decay and abandonment in the twentieth century.

For many years the abandoned canal lay derelict and forgotten. It hardly merited a mention in the history books of Chippenham and today the name 'Canal Road' on Pewsham housing estate is the only obvious reminder of its previous existence. It was only when the Wilts & Berks Canal Trust started to restore the canal that a new enthusiasm developed and people realised that an important industrial relic from two hundred years ago was re-awakening. In this book we explore the area, rediscovering small glimpses of the canal, and uncover the long forgotten history.

Map of the Wilts and Berks Canal, showing links to other towns and the wider canal network.

But as we enjoy the new found canal perhaps it is important to remember its original purpose and those who worked on it. The following pages record the development of the canal around Chippenham including the local Landowners and town leaders who had the confidence and vision to invest both time and money to make

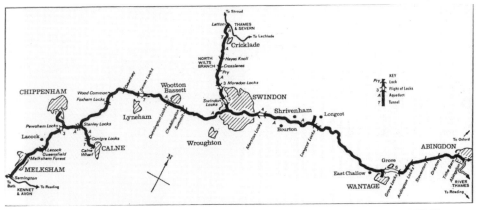

the canal possible. Of course there were also the people who worked and lived both on and alongside the canal. In capturing the ordinary citizens of Chippenham and the surrounding villages we discover how the canal initially brought prosperity to their lives, but as the canal network started to struggle, against increasing competition, so they suffered increasing hardship.

What brought the canal to Chippenham? Like most progress it was driven by trade and the promise of profits to be made. Canals were developed to support the increasing demands of the Industrial Revolution. As a comparison between canal and road transport of the eighteenth century, a boat on the canal could carry several tens of tons usually powered by a single horse. whereas the alternative of carts and pack horses could move only a few hundredweight, often along poorly maintained roads and track ways.

Chippenham in the eighteenth century was developing a thirst for raw materials. Industrial processes, such as steam driven textile mills, were introduced during the first decade of the nineteenth century, and the town became one of the biggest importers of canal borne coal along the Wilts & Berks.

Of course Chippenham's location, between the great trading cities of Bristol and London and within easy reach of Bath, also influenced the decision to bring the canal to the town. Until the canal age the only alternative to road transport between London and Bristol was by sea. This journey was both lengthy and hazardous, especially around Lands End. So it was not surprising there was so much support for the canal. Phillips in his Inland Navigation of 1792 said

> The utility of this canal (The Western Canal) from it's going through such a great scope of country, and through so many principal manufacturing towns, and also uniting the cities of London and Bristol, cannot but be of the greatest consequence both to the merchant and manufacturer, from the ease, cheapness and certainty of water-carriage in a few days from one city to the other.

Chippenham's traders saw the benefits and prosperity of a modern canal in the town, and many of them decided it was potentially such a successful venture that they subscribed to the canal companies.

2 Planning the Canal

The idea of connecting Bristol and London by waterway was suggested as early as the sixteenth century, but it was not until the 1760s that the first serious proposal was made to link the two cities. As part of this scheme in 1765 Ferdinando Stratford, an Engineer from Gloucester, presented a proposal for a 'Navigation between Bath and Chippenham' to the Society of Merchants in Bristol. His idea was to make use of the River Avon, but to introduce sections of canal to avoid mills and shallow areas of the river.[1]

The Bath and Chippenham canal proposal was never developed, but in 1788 an alternative was tabled. A meeting of interested landowners, including John Noyes Jnr, the Chippenham Bailiff[2], was held in Hungerford to promote the building of a Bristol to London 'Navigation'. It was agreed that the proposal had value and by November 1790 at a meeting in Marlborough the following resolution was made:

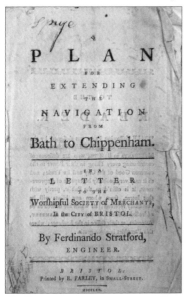

Pamphlet explaining Stratford's proposed plan for the Bath to Chippenham Navigation

That a Junction of the rivers Kennet & Avon by a canal navigation from Newbury to Bath by Hungerford Ramsbury Marlborough, and the Cheril lower level under White Horse Hill and through Calne and Chippenham Laycock Melksham and Bradford at the estimated expense of £213,940 is practicable and will be highly useful and beneficial to the subscribers and to the Publick at large.

This Canal scheme became known as the 'Western Canal'. Members of the Canal planning committee included amongst others Matthew Humphries or Humphrys, Ralph Hale Gaby and Lackham's

---

1   Wiltshire and Swindon Archives (WSA) 109/892, Ferdinando Stratfords plan for Navigation from Bath to Chippenham.
2   Goldney F H, Records of Chippenham

James Montague, landowners and town leaders from Chippenham.[3]. So confident was the town that land had been set aside for the building of the Canal, and the Chippenham Borough Account Book shows several payments to Mr Gaby for rent of land in anticipation of the Western Canal's arrival.

In August 1793 there was a change of heart. After several surveys it was decided to abandon the original route, in favour of a more southerly, and supposedly £20,000 cheaper, course through Great Bedwyn and Devizes[4]. This meant Chippenham and Calne no longer lay on the route of the proposed canal. There is a suggestion that cost was not the only reason for this change in route, in fact there is a doubt that the alternative plan truly was cheaper. A view was taken that there was a powerful voice in the county, the merchants and town council of Devizes, who wanted the economic advantage that the canal would bring. The two Devizes MPs lobbied hard on behalf of the town and perhaps some deals were made[5] to entice the canal, now known as Kennet & Avon,[6] to Devizes.

The compromise for Chippenham and Calne was that a branch would be cut linking them to the main line of the canal near Devizes. This would have meant a branch of over ten miles to get to Chippenham, making Chippenham a backwater on the canal and losing all the passing trade. Although not recorded it seems likely that Chippenham objected to these changes.

Western Canal meeting of 29 July 1788 held in Marlborough. At this meeting the committee were appointed Several of the members came from Chippenham

Proposal for the Wilts & Berks Canal

Whatever the reason for the change, all was not lost for Chippenham. In January 1793, possibly in anticipation of the changes on the Kennet & Avon, an announcement appeared in the Bath Chronicle calling for a meeting of all interested parties to consider a proposal for a canal to be built linking Bristol and Abingdon. This would provide an alternative route to meet the Thames and of course

---

3   WSA 109/893 Minutes of Western canal.
4   WSA 1644/28 Minutes of Western canal
5   Waylen, J, Chronicles of the Devizes 1839.
6   Evening Post February 1794: The Wilts & Berks committee meeting of 16 January 1794 refers to the Kennet & Avon.

another route to London. Importantly the proposal would again bring Chippenham into the canal network.

The meeting was held at Wootton Bassett on 30 January 1793 and no doubt Chippenham representatives, including Messrs Gaby, Montague and Humphries were present at the formation of this potentially lucrative venture. Certainly Mr Gaby was listed as one of the early subscribers to the Canal venture. The Bath Chronicle reported on the meeting of the proposed canal, later named The Wilts & Berks, and said:

> It will be of the greatest advantage to the Landed and Commercial interests of this County by opening a regular, safe and certain water carriage between all the towns and places near or adjoining such intended Canal from Bristol to or near Abingdon and from thence (by means of the Thames) to London.

Ralph Hale Gaby (left) and John Noyes Jnr as seen at the Yelde Hall Historic Council Chamber Chippenham. Both Gaby and Noyes were subscribers to the Wilts and Berks Canal.

To support the case for the canal Messrs Hall and Hughes were commissioned to prepare a survey of estimated trading figures for the Wilts & Berks Canal. From this report they expected the main commodity transported to be Somerset coal and estimated a saving of six shillings per ton at Chippenham over coal carried by road.

Planning and Negotiations

For the canal to become a reality a Bill setting out the proposal had to be laid before Parliament and only when the subsequent Act of Parliament had been passed could work to build the canal start. In preparing the Bill the Canal Committee met with landowners along the planned route to gain their support. By 1794 it had been decided that the route would terminate at a junction with the Kennet & Avon canal between Trowbridge and Devizes.

The Canal representatives attended a meeting of Chippenham Borough on the 8 February 1794 and explained that they proposed to build a branch from the main course of the canal to reach the town. To achieve this they would need to cross Englands, land owned by the Borough. Therefore the Canal Company sought 'consent and approval to the scheme and permission to bring the Canal through Borough Lands'.

The Corporation saw the value that a canal would bring to the town and agreed to the request of the Canal Company. The Borough minute book records the following:

> . . it appears that the said collateral branches will come through the Close of Land called Inglands belonging to this Borough and it being necessary that the Consent of the Corporation should be given to the said Canal previous to the presenting the Petition to Parliament.

Not only did the burgesses consent to the plan but they obviously felt it to be a sound investment, as they recorded their intention to subscribe to as many shares as regulation allowed.

The Canal Company also needed to negotiate with other landowners to gain permission to build the canal across their land. Much of the land needed for the Chippenham branch and part of Pewsham Forest was owned by Sir Samual Fludyer, son of the late Mayor of London. Mr Montague of Lackham owned land at Bowden Hill, Lacock and Pewsham. The stretch from Forest Gate to Stanley was in the ownership of the Baynton family of Spye Park. In Chippenham the Canal Company would later approach Harvey Head, Thomas Hall, Henry Guy and Ralph Gaby for agreement to bring the canal through their 'gardens' in Wood Lane.

Ivy House Chippenham. Residence of Matthew Humphries

Not surprisingly some of the landowners that the Canal Company negotiated with to build the canal were also shareholders in the company. This was true of both Ralph Hale Gaby and James Montague, both 'founding fathers' of the canal venture. They were also principal officers of the Wilts & Berks Canal Company. Amongst his duties Gaby was responsible for agreeing land valuations on behalf of the company[7]. while Montague was the Company Treasurer.

The business relationships did not stop there. In April 1792 Gaby and Montague along with two other partners, Matthew Humphrys of The Ivy in Chippenham and Robert Ash of Langley Burrell formed a bank in Chippenham.[8] This bank, known as Montague's bank, was closely linked with the canal during the final years of the eighteenth century recording entries for subscriptions to the 'Wilts & Berks Canal'

---

7   WSA 2424/50 Wilts & Berks records of vendors of land.
8   The formation of the bank was announced in the Bath Chronicle April 1792.

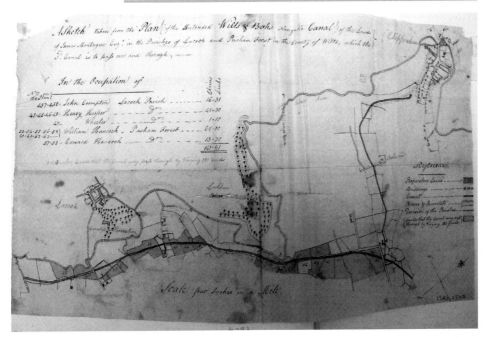

Extract from James Montague's map of 1793 showing the proposed Chippenham Branch

and the 'Western Canal'[9].When Montague died in 1797 Matthew Humphrys took over as treasurer of the Canal Company. Humphrys had also been at those early meetings of the Western Canal and no doubt like Gaby and Montague was prominent in the development of the Wilts & Berks.

It is clear that Chippenham produced a group of businessmen who in the latter years of the eighteenth century had a great deal of influence on the canal, not only in the town and surrounding area but also within the company itself.

These were influential men in the County. Matthew Humphrys and James Montague both held the appointment of High Sheriff of Wiltshire[10] while Ralph Hale Gaby held the title of Bailiff of Chippenham[11].

Letter from Matthew Humphreys Treasurer of the Wilts and Berks to Lord Radnor. The letter is addressed Ivy House,

---

9   Univ. London, Senate House Library, MS580, Account book for Montagues bank transcribed by Tony Pratt.

10 Annual Register 1792

11 Goldney, Records of Chippenham: Gaby was Bailiff in 1798, 1812 and 1816

3. Building the Canal

In September 1794, having gained the necessary agreements, the Canal Committee published a notice in the London Gazette of their intention to seek an Act of Parliament for 'making and maintaining a navigable Canal and Communication for Boats and Barges'. This notice listed the route of the canal and described the Chippenham section as :

Seal of the Wilts and Berks

> . . . In a Close or Ground in the Parish of Chippenham in the said County of Wilts called or known by the name of The Little Middle Ground in the occupation of John Lawes.

The resulting Bill received Royal Assent on 30 April 1795, and work started almost immediately. The Canal Company had already appointed Robert Whitworth and his son William to survey the canal and they would now act as engineers to oversee the building of the canal.

Unlike the Kennet & Avon canal the Wilts & Berks was to be a narrow canal, with a maximum boat width of seven foot.[12] A narrow boat meant less carrying capacity, but there were several arguments in favour of a narrow canal. One of these was that the bulk of traffic expected would be coal from Somerset, transported along the Somerset Coal Canal, also planned as a narrow canal.

A more compelling argument however, was that of cost. A narrow canal meant less digging out, narrower locks and smaller bridges, and more importantly less water was needed to maintain the canal.

In 1794, engineer Robert Whitworth calculated there was sufficient water supply available to maintain the narrow canal and 'provided a positive report and recommendation to the Gentleman subscribers to the proposed Wiltshire and Berkshire Canal'.[13]

---

12 London Evening Post Report of General Committee meeting at the Crown Inn Swindon 30 August 1794

13 Lawton, B, Building the Wilts & Berks p295. Lawton refers to a report in the Crowdy Letter Book

Robert Whitworth gave his first progress report later in 1795. He reported that the canal route was marked out from the junction with the Kennet & Avon at Semington as far as the Chippenham to Calne Turnpike road, now the A4 at Pewsham. He had also marked out six locks, three of which would be at Pewsham.

It was decided that as the local clay was suitable for brick making, bricks for locks and bridges should be made in the vicinity of the canal. Whitworth, therefore, proposed four brick yards, one of these being at Pewsham Forest. The number of bricks needed was staggering. Whitworth estimated he would need at least one million bricks from Pewsham Forest brickyard alone. He decided the bricks should be larger than the standard. This meant fewer bricks were needed – 700 bricks would do the same job as 1000 standard bricks. By using fewer bricks Whitworth argued that he would save on Brick Tax.[14] These large 'canal' bricks have also been found in cottages in Wood Lane suggesting that the Forest Brickworks was supplying the local community as well as the canal. Whitworth also placed advertisements locally for bricks and excavating the canal. The Salisbury and Winchester Journal of December 1796 contained the following advertisement for the Stanley stretch of the canal:

ELEVATION (PRESENT)

FROM CALNE

TO CHIPPENHAM

Plan and Elevation of Derry Hill Bridge. Wiltshire County Council 1914.

Two millions of bricks wanted, requesting proposals from any person desirous of contracting for the Digging Puddling and Compleating of the line of the Canal.

By 1797 the canal had reached Melksham, but there had been problems further north, at Pewsham Forest where several land slips had occurred meaning extra work was needed to strengthen the canal banks. Otherwise Whitworth reported all was going to plan. The three locks at Pewsham were well in hand. The bridge at Forest Gate Pewsham, which allowed the canal to pass under the Chippenham to Calne Turnpike road, was also completed during 1797. This substantial brick bridge, also known as Derry Hill Bridge, was built by the company of John Smith and John Bosville.[15]

14 Lawton, Building the Wilts & Berks, p299.
15 Dalby,.L J, The Wilts & Berks Canal p18; WSA 2424/27 Ledgers

Setbacks

The following year Robert Whitworth died and William, his son, provided the annual report in December 1798. He reported the main course of the canal had progressed towards Dauntsey. Land slippage at Pewsham Forest, near Lackham, was still troublesome and more piling was needed to maintain the canal sides. The branches to both the Calne and Chippenham were complete, but of course could not be used until the main line of the canal from Semington was complete.

During the next year, 1799, the positive news was that the three locks at Pewsham were complete. The cost amounted to about £180 per lock, with the top lock being £20 more because of the addition of a footbridge. The bad news was that the land slippages at Pewsham were still causing a problem and therefore were costing more than anticipated to resolve. These were minor problems however, compared with William Whitworth's other news for the canal committee.

Whitworth had checked the calculations for expected water supply to the canal. These were the calculations that allowed his father confidently to tell the Canal Company in 1794 that there was sufficient water for the canal. Unfortunately Whitworth found that his father's estimates were flawed; there simply wasn't enough water to maintain the canal[16]. Extra money would need to be found to provide sufficient water supply.

So the Wilts & Berks Canal Company approached the new century with serious financial problems. Whitworth's report of 1800 confirmed how serious the Wilts & Berks financial situation was. The canal was already £17500 over estimate.[17]

The Chippenham Arm

As the Chippenham Arm was now complete negotiations could take place to agree the value of Borough Land taken to construct the canal and towpath. In December 1798 John Noyes (Snr), William Ross and Revd William Weaver were appointed by Chippenham Borough to form a committee to negotiate with the Canal Company. The Borough minutes gave the following authority:

> to confer on behalf of the Borough with the representatives of the Committee of Management of the canal to ascertain the quantity

---

16 Dalby, Wilts & Berks Canal p21
17 Ibid.

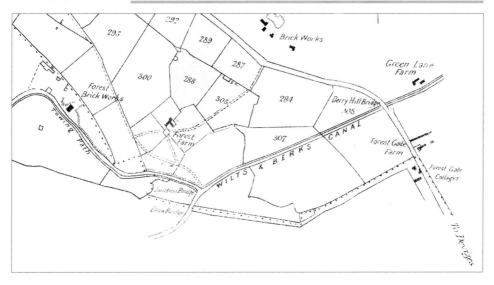

*Map showing
Chippenham junction
and bridge.*

of land taken and the damage done by the making of the said canal through the Borough lands.

The Borough records of April 1799 reported that an assessment had been made of the amount of land taken to build the canal and towpath. This was in excess of two acres, valued at £229 10s.0d. In addition more than an acre of land was deemed spoiled, damage caused when building the canal.

The account was submitted to the Canal Company but they were slow to pay. By May 1800 there were still monies outstanding and a dispute had developed about further land taken without consent. The Canal Company were hauling material and goods over this land, without permission and causing damage. Furthermore they were also illegally storing materials on Borough Lands. The Town Council obviously felt they needed to take a tough stance with the Canal Company as the Bailiff was empowered

> to demand such sum of the Treasurer of the Canal Company and until payment thereof to prevent the said Canal Company.... entering on the Borough Land and Passing and re passing to and from the Canal.

It appears that relations between the Town Council and the Canal Company continued to deteriorate and the corporation sent a deputation to Shrivenham to demand payment from the Canal Company. Thomas Goldney and the Bailiff were instructed by the corporation:

to wait upon the Committee of the Wilts & Berks Canal Co. to obtain an Order for the Payment of the Money due to the Borough for the Canal coming through Englands.

The Borough records of 1806 make it quite clear that the Bailiff and Mr Goldney were to take no nonsense from the Wilts & Berks Canal Company and were instructed to tell the Canal Committee that any sign of refusal or delay in payment would result in 'proceedings in law being taken against them for recovery of the same'. It appears that payment was eventually received.

Extract from Chippenham Bailiffs book listing part of the final amount due to the corporation from the Canal Company for land used to build the canal.

Further setback and the Chippenham tunnel

There was further setback for the Canal Company during 1799. Both Calne and Chippenham Town Councils disputed that the Canal branches terminated in the correct location. Chippenham Borough maintained that the Act of 1795 required the canal to terminate closer to the centre of the town, and therefore said the canal needed to be extended. William Whitworth, directed that any work to extend the branches should be suspended pending a full investigation. He recognised that the cost of the Canal was already spiralling and extending the branches, as required by the Town councils, would only compound the problems of the Canal Company.

The Borough Council of Chippenham argued that the 1795 Act specified that the Chippenham Branch should terminate within one hundred yards of the town. Their complaint was that the town consisted of 500 houses, but the Branch of the canal, terminating in 'The Common Meadow called Englands' was at a greater distance from the town centre, with only fifteen outlying cottages being within the specified 100 yards.

On 4th July 1800 the Borough Council agreed to resolve this dispute by appointing a referee to represent them. Accordingly the Bailiff and Burgesses appointed Daniel Clutterbuck of Bradford to act on their behalf. The Canal Company, represented by John Awdry and Ralph Hale Gaby, had already appointed their referee, a Gentleman by the name of Caleb Dickenson of Pickwick Lodge, Corsham. It was agreed that Clutterbuck and Dickenson would in turn appoint an independent adjudicator to help 'determine the said question'. The adjudicator nominated was Sir Charles Warre Malet, of Hartham Park near Corsham.

Having visited the town, taken measurements, and heard from witnesses, the two referees and adjudicator gave their decision to the Town Council on 15 July 1800. The decision was that the Canal Company did not comply and could not comply with the intent of the Act. This meant it was the responsibility of the Canal Company to extend the branch closer to the town, and Whitworth, after considering several options, decided to lengthen the canal for it to terminate in Timber Street, within a few yards of the Market Place.

This decision provided Whitworth with a further problem however. The new terminus would be on the far side of a ridge of high ground and the only realistic option was to build a 90 yard tunnel under 'John Simpkin's garden' in Wood Lane. Work to build the tunnel, and the additional 540 yards of canal[18] started in 1800 and was finally completed in 1803. At the same time the new wharf in Timber Street was completed.

Although this was a victory for the town some of the Burgesses (members of the council), must have had mixed feelings. When the decision was made to appoint Daniel Clutterbuck to represent the borough, the decision was taken by, amongst others, John Noyes Snr, John Noyes Jnr, William Taylor and William Tarrant. As Burgesses they had a duty to ensure that the town was properly represented in the dispute, but they had a dilemma. As well as being representatives of the Borough they were also subscribers in the Canal Company. They had speculated in the Company, considering it to be a sound proposition, and now they were voting against their investments, in the knowledge that a decision against the Wilts & Berks would push it further into debt.

More investment and a new Act of Parliament

As expected, the Wilts & Berks fell into greater debt. The tunnel dispute of course was just the latest in a number of setbacks and the Company needed to find extra funds urgently. The only option was for the committee to petition for a further Act of Parliament which would allow them to raise more money. In June 1801 the following notice appeared in the London Gazette:

18 Lawton, Building the Wilts & Berks p300

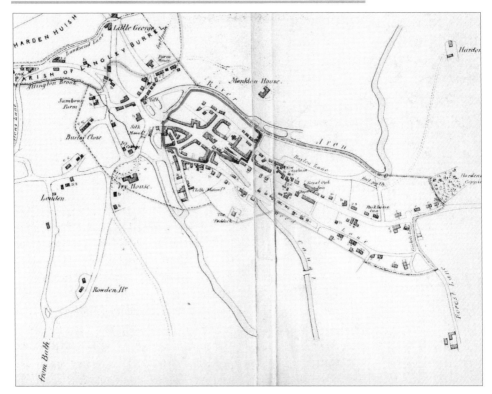

An Act for enabling the Company of Proprietors of the Wilts & Berks Canal Navigation to raise money for completing the said canal; and to alter, explain and amend the Act passed in the Thirty-fifth year of the reign of His Present Majesty for making the said canal.

Map of 1831 showing the canal entering Chippenham. The Wharf is top centre and the tunnel that was built as a result of the disputed location of the canal can be seen at the centre of the map. The road above the tunnel is Wood Lane.

The reference to 'explaining' the Act meant that the resolved dispute over the Chippenham arm would be included in the new Act. The 1801 Act now quite clearly contained a description of where the canal was to terminate and included the following sentence to avoid any doubt: '. . . to terminate in or near the site of a dwelling house and gardens belonging to Ralph Hale Gaby'.

To raise the additional funds as approved by the Act, further shares were offered to subscribers. Newspapers, such as Jackson's Oxford Journal, contained notices declaring the share offer during the autumn of 1801. The closing date for the share issue was 12 December 1801 and payments were to be sent to Matthew Humphrys, Treasurer, Ivy House Chippenham.

4. The Canal in Use

Despite the disputed location of the terminus, the Chippenham Branch had been navigable since 1800[19] and an increasing number of barges were carrying goods to and from the town. The borough records of 30 June 1801 resolved that a charge of two shillings would be levied on all Barge masters loading or unloading a barge at Englands. Messrs Goldney & Hall were regular carriers at Chippenham and the Borough accounts show they were charged £2 at Michaelmas (29 September) 1801 for loading or unloading 20 barges in Englands.

In addition to the loading and unloading of barges, Englands was also the site for boat building. Messrs Henry Guy and Co. were charged five Guineas per year for land they occupied to build boats and a further two and a half Guineas per year to load and unload boats, and haulage to and from the canal.[20]. Another boat builder in the area was John Provis, the Chippenham Timber Merchant. When he finally retired in 1841 the catalogue[21] for the sale of his business included 3 canal boats, 5000 feet of 2 inch boat plank and 1000 boat knees.

It had always been anticipated that coal would be the principal commodity to be transported on the canal. The Canal Company report of 1802 was very positive saying:

> The demand for Somerset Coal had now become very great on the line of the Wilts & Berks Canal. . . Such is the superior quality of this coal there is no doubt that it will be carried to the east end of the canal and beyond.

This optimism was further supported when the Somerset Coal Canal was completed in 1805, providing a continuous canal route from the Somerset Coal fields, via the Kennet & Avon Canal to the Wiltshire

---

19   Jacksons Oxford Journal reported that the canal was navigable from Semington to Chippenham, Calne and Wootton Bassett.
20   Chippenham Museum and Heritage Centre: Chippenham Bailiff book 1801.
21   Devizes and Wiltshire Gazette March 1841.

towns. The increasing demand for Somerset coal was reflected in Chippenham. In fact by 1838 Chippenham was second only to Abingdon in the tonnages unloaded.[22]

Of course it was not only coal that was transported on the waterway. In 1830, twenty years after the completion of the canal, Joseph Priestley published his Navigable Rivers and Canals, where he said that corn, stone and cheese, in addition to coal, were also carried on the Wilts & Berks. The records show that corn and produce such as potatoes were carried on the canal. Stone was regularly brought along the canal from the quarries around Bath. However in reality, very little cheese was moved by canal, the cheese makers preferring road and later rail transport[23].

Locally, at Pewsham, hurdles were collected and shipped around the district.[24] Timber was another commodity regularly carried on the canal, and auctioneers would highlight the value of the nearby canal, when advertising the sale of standing wood. An advert from 1806 for the sale of woodland in Bremhill, Bowood and Calne said 'This timber is well suited for either water or land carriage . . the Wilts & Berks canal being nearby'.

Boats on the canal. An, engraving from The Illustrated London News of the mid nineteenth century. This is a typical scene and probably reflected life on the Chippenham Arm.

Completion of the Canal and signs of prosperity

In 1805 Whitworth was able to provide a positive report and confirmed that the Wilts & Berks was navigable as far as Swindon. Work continued during the following years and gradually the canal headed into Berkshire. Finally five years later on 14th September 1810, the Wilts & Berks Canal was completed. It had cost more and taken longer to build than anticipated, but despite this the opening of the canal into the Thames was celebrated at Abingdon with a banquet, music and speeches.

22   Dalby, L J, The Wilts & Berks Canal Appendix 5.
23   Wilson, A, Forgotten Harvest p96. Wilson says that there was reluctance by local cheesemakers to use the canal.
24   WSA 2424/45: Toll ledgers.

REDUCED PRICE OF CARRIAGE,

BY THE

Wilts and Berks
CANAL COMPANY,

TO AND FROM

London and Bristol.

BOATS will set out weekly, with or without a full Freight, from the *Three Cranes and Hambro' Wharfs*, Queen Street, LONDON, and from the *Wilts and Berks Wharf*, Temple Back, BRISTOL.

Wharfs where Goods are received, and Wharfingers Names.

LONDON,	Three Cranes and Hambro' Wharfs,	Messrs. SILLS, RAMSAY, and GRAY.
ABINGDON,	Canal Wharf,	MR. J. PRINCE.
WANTAGE,	Ditto	MR. S. PLUMBE.
LONGCOT,	Ditto	MR. J. CARTER.
SWINDON,	Ditto	MR. J. CANN.
WOOTTON-BASSET,	Ditto	MR. J. GARDINER.
DANTSEY,	Ditto	Messrs. HOPKINS.
CALNE,	Ditto	MR. ATCHLEY.
CHIPPENHAM,	Ditto	MR. WHARRY.
LACOCK,	Ditto	MR. C. PETTIFER.
MELKSHAM,	Ditto	MR. D. MULCOCK.
BATH,	Sydney Wharf,	MR. R. CLARKE.
BRISTOL,	Wilts and Berks Wharf, Temble Backs,	MR. T. HOWE.

N. B. Goods intended for Oxford, Witney, Banbury, Burford, and other parts of the North of England, are regularly forwarded from Abingdon.

There are regular Passage Boats twice a Week, from the Canal Wharf, ABINGDON, to the Wilts and Berks Wharf, Sydney Gardens, BATH.

BAILY, Printer, Binder, &c. Post-Office, CALNE.

Advert for weekly carriage service In 1814. The charge for general goods from London to Chippenham was £1, 13s, 6d per ton.

This meant that Chippenham was now linked directly to London. A boat could leave the town and travel the Wilts & Berks to Abingdon. From Abingdon the Thames took the boat into the heart of the capital. Equally exciting were the opportunities in the opposite direction with boats being able to reach Bristol via the Kennet & Avon canal and the River Avon. Adverts soon appeared for 'Water carriage between Bristol and London'. This was a regular service from Three Cranes and Hambro' Wharfs, London, to Bristol, calling at amongst others Chippenham Wharf.[25]

Although the Wilts & Berks Canal Company was celebrating the linking of Bristol and London by waterway, it was in direct competition with the Kennet & Avon Canal Company. There had already been disputes with the Kennet & Avon about access through Bath locks to the Somerset Coal Canal and there had been some debate as to which was the more economic route.

The original proposal for the Wilts & Berks was to link Bristol to Abingdon and then by Thames into London. This had only partially been achieved as the Wilts & Berks were still reliant on the Kennet & Avon to complete the journey to Bristol. Therefore, in May 1810 a meeting was held at the Angel Inn in Chippenham[26] to propose the cutting of a canal from the City of Bristol to a junction of the Wilts & Berks at Foxham, north of Chippenham.

This was a major threat to the Kennet & Avon and it appears that its supporters attempted to disrupt the meeting. The newspaper report of the time said, 'at the meeting on Saturday at Chippenham a very novel proceeding was resorted to by an interested party, to prevent the object of it being carried out.'

25 London Gazette 20 March 1814: Notice of weekly boats between London and Bristol through the Wilts & Berks Canal.
26 Jacksons Oxford Journal.

The Kennet & Avon Company issued leaflets disputing the positive claims made for the Wilts &Berks and the proposed junction canal. The meeting became quite heated and when Mr Hallett, the Chairman of the management committee of the Wilts & Berks, stood to give his address. He said, 'The Kennet & Avon is a rival canal and the Proprietors were with very good cause jealous of the high and superior estimation in which the Wilts & Berks is held'. He went on to say that 'the Kennet & Avon Company had by their insinuations attempted to prejudice the public mind'. The public clearly were not swayed by the Kennet & Avon and the subscribers flocked to sign the subscription paper.

The Angel Inn, Chippenham

In September 1810 notice was given in the London Gazette of the intention to apply to Parliament for a Bill for the Bristol Junction Canal. A bill was introduced in 1810 but withdrawn the next year.[27] Perhaps the Kennet & Avon eventually succeeded in swaying the public.

In 1810 a pamphlet was published by Mr Mayo of Newbury entitled A Comparative Statement Relative to The Kennet & Avon and Wilts & Berks lines of communication between London and Bristol. This was an in-depth comparison between the two canals, considering which was the best value. The conclusion favoured the Kennet & Avon over the Wilts & Berks. There is a temptation to suggest that Mayo was biased in favour of the Kennet & Avon. It flowed through Newbury, and he probably had business interests in the town. He did however raise a vital argument. The fact the Wilts & Berks was a narrow canal, which in turn meant boats were limited to a maximum of 25 to 30 tons carrying capacity. The wider Kennet & Avon allowed larger boats carrying up to sixty tons and Mayo argued that for this reason they were more efficient making the Kennet & Avon a cheaper route. This was an argument that continued to haunt the Wilts & Berks throughout the rest of its life.

Mayo's Comparative Statement Relative the Kennet and Avon and Wilts and Berks Canal

Railway competition

The Wilts & Berks never did reach the levels of profit anticipated in the Hall and Hughes report,

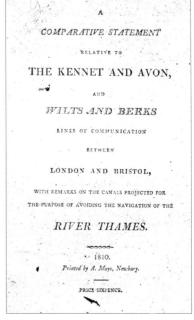

27 www.jim-shead.com/waterways

although for the first thirty years trade grew steadily. Tolls charged in 1812 amounted to £5,765 and by 1840 they had increased to £24001.[28]

With the completion of the Great Western Railway between London and Bristol in 1841, and locally the opening of Chippenham Station, competition from the railway saw trade on the canal decline. Ironically one of the most prosperous periods for the canal was during the eighteen thirties and forties, transporting stone and materials to build bridges and buildings for the Great Western Railway Company. Much of the stone for the railway village and locomotive works in Swindon was moved from Bath using the Wilts & Berks.

The Somerset coal trade was not immediately affected by the advent of the railway age. It would be some years before the railway links were established between the coalfields and the Wiltshire towns, however; the opening of the Wilts, Somerset & Weymouth Railway Junction at Thingley in 1848, with its proximity to Chippenham,

WILTS & BERKS CANAL LESSEES,
Canal Carriers & Warehousemen,
GENERAL CARRIERS
Of Merchandise and Goods To and From

Bristol	Wootton Bassett,	Cricklade,
Bath	Hay Lane,	Devizes,
Bradford,	Swindon,	Hungerford,
Hilperton.	Bourton,	Aldermaston,
(For Trowbridge).	Uffington	Theale,
Semington,	(For Faringdon),	Migham.
Melksham,	Shrivenham,	Reading,
Lacock,	Challow.	Stroud,
Chippenham,	Longcott,	Gloucester,
Calne. .	Wantage,	&c., &c., or any
Foxham,	Abingdon,	intermediate
Dauntsey,	Oxford,	Wharf.

Advertisement for canal carriers listing the towns served. Towns included those on the Kennet and Avon.

heralded the beginning of the railway takeover.

In 1857 William Fox Talbot of Lacock Abbey was in correspondence with a Mr Coombes concerning the sale of Iron Ore found at Nethermore, near Lacock. Fox Talbot proposed using the nearby Wilts & Berks canal to ship the Ore to Staffordshire, but Mr Coombes replied suggesting rail transport would be cheaper, a sign of the increasing competition from the railway. It is not known if Fox Talbot ever made use of the canal.[29]

28 Dalby, Wilts & Berks Canal Appendix 3
29 Talbot Correspondence Project http://foxtalbot.dmu.ac.uk

5. Decline and Decay

Despite the increasing competition from the Great Western Railway, Chippenham and nearby Stanley wharf remained major destinations of Somerset coal into the second half of the nineteenth century. In fact demand was such that tonnages of canal borne coal continued to increase year on year, peaking in 1854 when nine and a half thousand tons was delivered to these wharves.[30]

In the same year that coal figures peaked at Chippenham and Stanley, the Wilts, Somerset and Weymouth Railway Company completed their branch line between Frome and Radstock.[31] This meant that there was now a rail link from the Somerset coal fields through Frome, Westbury, Trowbridge, Melksham and Thingley Junction to Chippenham.

The impact was immediate and Chippenham saw a rapid decline in the amount of coal delivered by canal. By 1878 a mere 1,745 tons was received at Chippenham, less than 20% of the 1854 figure. Of course Chippenham was not alone. The picture was repeated across the length of the canal and the company was helpless as it saw profit levels fall. Profit levels were so poor that in 1871 no dividend was paid to shareholders; in fact, the company continued to struggle financially for the following forty years.

Toll Permit dated 20 August 1860. This boat was carrying twenty eight and a half tons of coal to Dauntsey. The Master was John Teagle who it is thought came from the Christian Malford area.

30 Dalby, Wilts & Berks Canal
31 Great Western Society Bristol Group www.r.heron.btinternet.co.uk

Maintaining the canal

As profits fell so the Canal Company looked to saving money and no doubt repairs and maintenance were subject to close scrutiny. Certainly there were reports of bridges and locks being neglected and the canal soon fell into disrepair.

Chippenham felt the effect of this neglect and in 1880 the Town Clerk was forced to write to the company about the continued flooding of Little England's caused by leaks in the canal. The town records show that the council were in no doubt that the Canal Company were wholly responsible to repair the leaks, but realised there was little likelihood of them meeting their obligations, so reluctantly the Town Council authorised £20 for repairs. The canal had been leaking for some time and as the leaks grew more serious, so the area started suffering landslips. In all about 2 acres of Little Englands were affected, which were described by the Town Council as 'quite spoiled', in fact so spoiled that the 'Town Rifle Corps', who carried out their target practice in Englands, were forced to complain to the Town Council who eventually agreed to move the ranges to Westmead.

There were other reports of flooding, one of the most serious being at Chippenham wharf where, due to worn coping stones, the canal spilled over into the Market Place flooding several cellars.

The Town clerk continued to write to the Canal Company over the next few years about necessary repairs to the tunnel, bridges, gates and fences along the Chippenham branch of the canal. By 1892 the letters of complaint had become quite regular and the minute book showed the increasing frustration of the Council. The Town Clerk's persistence paid off eventually, as the minutes of August 1893 said that fences and the bridge had been repaired and tree felling had been carried out. This came as 'too little too late' however, as there was still a great deal left undone along the canal and a lot of investment was required just to bring the canal back to a reasonable standard.

The scale of the problem was highlighted in an article published in the Pall Mall Gazette called 'In Tow: some notes of a summer cruise in inland waterways'.[32] This was an account of a pleasure trip from Reading to Abingdon along the Kennet & Avon and Wilts & Berks canals during 1894. Before setting out the travellers were warned that the Wilts & Berks canal was in poor condition and they would have

---

32   Wilts & Berks Canal Trust: http://wabinfo.gentle-highway.info/in_tow. htm

difficulties navigating. The locks were described as dangerous and the lift bridges as troublesome. The author of the article was given the following advice

> Nothing but a common trade-boat will, at present, go up the Wilts & Berks Canal, as the bridges (wooden) are too low, and out of order; unless these were properly kept it would not be worth while making a boat to suit them.

The trip was successful however and by the fifteenth day they had arrived at Pewsham. The only comment made at Pewsham was, 'Canal agents residence. See remains of old section boats, on the right'.

In 1900 the Calne Borough council were equally scathing and reported that the Calne branch had been neglected for many years and had been allowed to silt up, to such an extent that that it was practically unnavigable and only light boats could pass through.[33] In Frank Heath's Wiltshire volume of the 'Little Guides' series published in 1901, he said: 'The canal is practically a thing of the past. Its stiffened and weedy waters are stirred only by the moor-hen who walks more than she swims across them.' The canal was so little used that all that knew her had christened her 'the deserted little Wilts & Berks Canal'.

Canal bridges were also declared unsafe for public use by the highway authorities, a particularly serious case being a footbridge at Bremhill that seemed to be on the point of collapse. The poor condition of the bridges became such a serious matter that in early February 1890 Mr Williams, the Clerk to the Chippenham Highway Board, was forced to apply to the Magistrates for an order against the Wilts & Berks Canal Company to repair Naish Hill Bridge in Lacock. At the court hearing Mr Pratt, from the Canal Company, asked for a month's adjournment and explained the company was in a 'state of transition'. The magistrates clearly saw this as an unreasonable request and made an order for the bridge to be repaired by 28 February[34].

Calls to close the canal

These problems were the culmination of years of neglect, but it was clear as early as 1874 that the future of the canal was in doubt and the idea of closing the canal had to be considered. To close a canal

---

33   WSA 918/132/42: Borough of Calne correspondence.
34   Bristol Mercury 7 February 1890

Brinkworth's 1877 advertisement. Although he recommended Canal borne coal he kept his options open by having a further yard at the railway station.

needed an Act of Parliament and this proposal was raised in the North Wilts Herald in September of that year.

At Chippenham, local landowners and traders met to discuss the closure of the canal, JC Townsend, (possibly John Townsend, brickmaker of Pewsham) said that the water levels in the canal were so low and locks and bridges so badly maintained that it had taken ten days to reach Wantage, a distance of under forty miles. Furthermore he said the high tolls charged meant the canal simply could not compete with the railways.[35]

Inevitably a bill was prepared proposing to close the canal, but a group of businessmen, several of them canal traders, agreed to buy the company and save the canal. It therefore transferred to the new owners in 1877 but retained the identity of the Wilts & Berks Canal. The new owners did everything possible to encourage new business but towards the end of the nineteenth century there was a further blow to the canal's future. It became apparent that the Somerset coalfields, the canal's major source of trade, were almost worked out. W H Brinkworth, coal merchant at Chippenham Wharf, valiantly soldiered on and tried to persuade his customers of the value of using the canal. His advertisement of 1877 gave the following recommendation. 'The best Somersetshire Coal which is obtainable only by Canal. The quality is superior to that had by rail.'

Despite Brinkworth's and the canal company's best efforts the reality that the canal would never become a commercial proposition

35   Wilts and Gloucester Standard January 1875

was realised by 1897 and a Warrant of Abandonment was applied for. This application was opposed by Swindon New Town and Wiltshire County Council. The Bristol Times and Mirror reported on the County Council meeting and gave as one of the main reasons for opposition the loss of water rights and water supply. The canal was an important source of water for farmers and their livestock, so it is not surprising that the application was opposed.

　　The subject of closure was raised at the Chippenham Urban Sanitary Authority meeting in May 1897. After some debate they also decided to oppose the closure of the canal. The minutes said there were various reasons for this opposition, but the main reason was that 'abandonment of means of water carriage [would] be disadvantageous to the public interest'. In support of retaining the canal Mr. Brinkworth, the Chippenham coal merchant, told the meeting that six boats a fortnight brought coal to the Wharf.[36] He did not mention whether the boats were fully laden!

MAY 8, 1897

CHIPPENHAM

CANAL: SHALL IT BE CLOSED?

At the monthly meeting of the Chippenham Urban Sanitary Authority, the Mayor presiding . . . the question of the proposed closure of the canal was discussed and the general opinion was against the proposed abandonment.

The Clerk said he had been informed by Mr Brinkworth that at Chippenham there were about six boats a fortnight, which brought to the Wharf about 520 tons of coal.

The Mayor added that in the rural district there were 66 boats registered last year as having passed along the canal, and 15 so far this year.

Newspaper report of the Chippenham Urban Sanitary Authority meeting of May 1897 where the proposed closure of the canal was discussed.

36　Chippenham Museum and Heritage Centre: Joe Buckle Scrapbook

6. Abandonment

In 1900 the Board of Trade opened an enquiry into the abandonment application. Feelings were running high between the syndicate representing the canal and local landowners. The landowners supported the view that the canal should remain open as it provided drainage and watering for cattle. The syndicate representing the canal felt it had no positive value and was simply a financial burden.

By August 1900 the County Council were considering a possible solution by taking over and maintaining the canal. They wrote to the local authorities asking for agreement that they would take over repair of bridges in their district. For Chippenham this would mean Englands bridge and the tunnel leading to the wharf.

In September 1900 the Town Clerk was asked to convene a meeting of the Town Council to discuss the County Council letter and to propose that it be accepted. There is no record that this meeting ever took place, but by February 1901 Wiltshire County Council had changed its mind and decided it would not adopt the canal, the reason given being, 'the importance of the canal as a traffic route was not sufficient to justify the acquisition of the canal'.[37]

The collapsed aqueduct at Stanley, photo taken mid 1960s.

Fate then stepped in. Between the junctions of the Chippenham and Calne branches the canal crossed Stanley Aqueduct, a substantial brick structure that crossed the River Marden. The aqueduct, like the rest of the canal, had suffered from years of neglect and was in poor condition, so it came as no great surprise when one stormy night early in 1901 a four foot section of an arch collapsed into the river and the canal simply drained away. The Canal Company did

37 Dalby. Wilts & Berks Canal p94.

not have the funds to repair the aqueduct and probably saw no reason to make any moves in that direction, as the damage could only help their case for abandonment.

Although the link between the Kennet & Avon and the Thames had been broken there was still some local traffic on the canal. By 1904 tolls collected amounted to mere £2 8s.6d.[38] A report on Waterways in Great Britain confirmed by 1906 the canal was derelict with grass growing at the bottom and the locks out of order.[39]

Complaints about the canal

In Chippenham there was little mention of the Canal until 1907 when a notice was served on the Secretary of the Canal Company 'to forthwith abate a nuisance in the neighbourhood of the Westmead Schools in Wood Lane'.[40] The nuisance was foul smells caused by the low level of the canal especially where drains flowed into it. The Secretary of the Canal Company responded to the notice by saying that he would raise the height of the water in the canal to solve the problem. In January 1908 the company surveyor attended 'to see if it is possible that water level can be maintained to prevent a nuisance'. It clearly was not, as in May 1912, the Borough Surveyor met with the Secretary of the Canal Company who suggested that the canal, from the Wharf to the tunnel be emptied of remaining stagnant water. The Borough Surveyor agreed to this solution and the result was that the smells vanished. Inevitably, the empty canal then became an unauthorised rubbish tip. Councillor Townsend raised the matter at the Chippenham Urban District Meeting in July 1912 and said that there was an infestation of rats in the vicinity of the canal. He did not say what the cause of the infestation might be, but it was known that offal and other foodstuff had been dumped in the canal. The Town Council also received a letter from Messrs Keary Stokes and White, Solicitors to the Gaby Estate, owners of the land surrounding the canal, reminding the Town Council of an agreement not to use the canal as a tip.[41] To avoid further complaints,

38 Dalby lists the Tolls in his book. By comparison Tolls for 1891 were £671 and 1837 were £12,887.

39 Institution of Civil Engineering Virtual library: Discussion, 32 On Waterways In Great Britain, www.icevirtuallibrary.com.

40 Chippenham Museum and Heritage Centre: Chippenham UDC minute book 7.

41 Chippenham Museum and Heritage Centre: Chippenham UDC minute book 8.

it was recommended to fill the canal completely, from the wharf to the tunnel, and make it level with the surrounding area . In 1916 the Council committee felt that getting rid of the canal was one of the greatest and most permanent sanitary improvements in the Borough for years.

As the canal between the wharf and the tunnel was being filled, the canal beyond the tunnel, in Englands, was also emptied of water. It was decided to make use of this stretch, as far as the borough boundary, as the official town tip. By April 1920, the old canal had been completely filled with refuse, and it was levelled and grass seed planted. In the 1980s the town tip was once again uncovered when excavation work took place for the construction of Pewsham Way. As the diggers cut through the tip so they unearthed hundreds of bottles from the early twentieth century. Local residents explored the works and collected the old bottles.

As the tip closed, in 1920, so the Town Council needed to provide a replacement and they decided to buy the canal beyond the borough boundary, probably as far as Jays Bridge, as an extension to the tip[42]. There were reports in 1926 of pig offal being illegally tipped in this section of the derelict canal[43]. It seems, however that this part of the canal was not used by the town as today the canal route can still be seen quite clearly running alongside Pewsham Way.

The WILTS AND BERKS CANAL COMPANY.
Swindon Corporation (Wilts and Berks Canal Abandonment) Act, 1914.

NOTICE is hereby given, that all persons having claims upon the Wilts and Berks Canal Company are required, in pursuance of the above Act, to furnish full particulars of the same to the Company at its principal office, at Central Chambers, Swindon, in the county of Wilts, forthwith, and in any event before the 2nd day of March, 1915; and notice is hereby also given, that on and after the said 2nd day of March, 1915, the Company will be at liberty to distribute the assets of the Company, or any part thereof, amongst the parties entitled thereto, having regard to the claims of which the Company then has notice.—Dated the 9th day of January, 1915.

For the Wilts and Berks Canal Company,
151   W. J. AINSWORTH, Secretary.

Canal Abandonment notice January 1915 from the London Gazette.

The Abandonment Act

Although Chippenham had already rid itself of the canal, it was not until 1914 that the canal was finally abandoned, when the Swindon Corporation (Wilts & Berks Canal Abandonment) Act received royal assent. The Act transferred Coate reservoir and the Swindon portion of the canal to the Borough of Swindon and allowed the remainder of the route to be disposed of, usually back to local landowners.

The Borough council again took ownership of the canal land in Englands and decided there was no need to maintain Englands bridge,

42   Chippenham Museum and Heritage Centre: Chippenham UDC minute book 10.
43   Chippenham Museum and Heritage Centre: Chippenham UDC minutes February 1926.

The derelict canal at Studley in 1956.. Stanley Aqueduct is in the trees in the centre of the picture.

Stanley Bridge today. The bridge has been demolished and the railings are the only sign the canal course is either side of the road. It is thought the bridge was demolished in the 1950s or 60s, although it was included in the 1914 survey by Wiltshire County Council

arranging for it to be demolished.[44] The remaining two bridges along the Chippenham Arm, Deep Cutting and Jay's bridge, were outside the town's authority and remained intact, well into the 1930s and probably later.

The bridges on the main line of the canal, Derry Hill, Studley and Stanley, became the responsibility of Wiltshire County Council

---

44 Chippenham Museum and Heritage Centre: Chippenham UDC minute books. There had been discussions with the Canal Company from 1912 to demolish Englands Bridge, and replace it with a level crossing.

Highways Department, as they were accountable for the upkeep of the roads. The Council did not want the burden of the bridges and carried out surveys in 1914, with the intention that the bridges should be demolished and the roads levelled. The bridges were levelled over the following years and today there is very little sign they ever existed.[45]

Chippenham wharf was sold at auction in 1915. The wharf itself was in the possession of the Gaby family, but the canal that cut through the wharf was owned by the canal company, making the sale of the wharf and surrounding land potentially complicated. However, when the abandonment of the canal took place in 1914 the title of the canal passed to George Alfred Huelin White, a solicitor of Chippenham. White and the Gaby family agreed to sell the wharf and canal as a single plot, and the auctioneer described it as 'A large Wharf yard particularly adapted for business purposes, there being sufficient area for the erection of a large factory or works'.

Finally, Chippenham's last link to the canal disappeared in 1971. A hundred and seventy years after the Chippenham tunnel was built it was decided it should be filled in and bricked up. The tunnel had been used as a rubbish tip for some years and was considered an eyesore and a nuisance. According to Mr Barnett,[46] the Highways Superintendent for Chippenham Borough, the tunnel was still partly in water, and before filling the tunnel with hardcore it took five days to pump the water out. Once filled the tunnel entrance was finally sealed. From Mr Barnett's description it appears that the tunnel mouth may still be in place but hidden in the undergrowth, close to the roundabout near the Magistrates court.

(top) A final inspection of Chippenham tunnel in 1971. Soon after the tunnel was sealed up. In the background can be seen accumulated rubbish

(above) The entrance to Chippenham tunnel before it was filled in 1971.

45   WSA F4/150/42: 1914 report on canal bridges.

46   Wiltshire Gazette 22 September 1994. Letter from Mr LG Barnett describing the filling in of the tunnel.

7. People and Places

The Canal Company kept meticulous records of boats travelling the canal, to ensure that tolls were correctly charged and payments subsequently received. Today these documents provide us with an invaluable picture of life on the canal, including the loads carried, the destination of each boat and the name of the master, also known as a steerer. One of these 'steerers' was Chippenham born James Bryant, who worked a boat owned by Brinkworth, the coal and builders merchant of Chippenham.

Detail from cover of Traders and Collectors ledger.

In early April 1881, fifty-six year old Bryant was moored at Camerton, on the Somersetshire Coal Canal, loaded with 24 tons of coal ready to return to Chippenham. Also on board was his 'mate', twenty-one year old Thomas Dorset or Dorsett of Melksham.[47] Camerton to Chippenham was a well worn path for Bryant and Dorset. It took over two days to cover the route and within the first three weeks of April they had delivered four loads of coal to Chippenham.[48]

Extract from the canal companies ledgers.

47   1881 Census.
48   WSA 2424/45: Canal Registers.

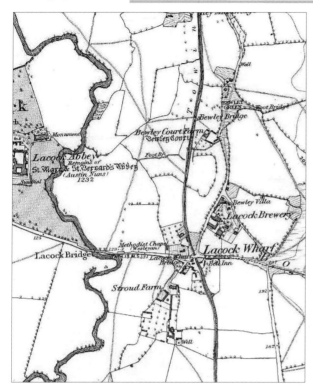

Ordnance Survey map showing Lacock Wharf and surrounding area in the 1880s.

Leaving Camerton Bryant and Dorset navigated the Somersetshire Coal Canal to join the Kennet & Avon close to Dundas Aqueduct. Once on the Kennet & Avon they headed eastward for Semington, the junction with the Wilts & Berks canal.

Lacock

At Semington, they joined the Wilts & Berks, Bryant registered his load and destination with the Toll Keeper, who in turn issued Bryant with a permit to travel the canal. The Canal Company ledgers confirm that he arrived at Semington on 5 April 1881 and his destination was Chippenham. The toll levied by the company was eight pence per ton so the charge for Bryant's twenty-four tons of coal was sixteen shillings.

From Semington Bryant headed northwards through Melksham to Lacock. Today there is little sign that a canal ever passed through Lacock, but in its heyday the village boasted a busy wharf. The wharf ran alongside the Bell Inn, on the outskirts of the village, where shipments, such as, timber, corn and building materials were delivered by canal. Bath stone was regularly brought to Lacock. The stone was unloaded from the boats using a crane with a pair of nippers or tongs attached to bite into the stone.[49]

James Bryant was no stranger to the wharf. When he was not bringing coal from Somerset he was employed by Mr Brinkworth to deliver bricks and pipes from Brinkworth's yard in Chippenham. But of course, like the other towns and villages along the Wilts & Berks canal, coal was the principal trade at Lacock. For over thirty years George Banks, who lived in the Wharf House, was the local coal merchant.

---

49   Talbot Correspondence Project http://foxtalbot.dmu.ac.uk. Charles Talbot April 1860.

When George died in the early 1880s his wife Elizabeth continued the business despite being well into her seventies.[50] George and Elizabeth's daughter Anna was also employed at the wharf. She was engaged as 'accountant at the Canal Wharf'. Her duties would have included maintaining records and receipts of transactions on behalf of the Canal Company.

In Peter Murray's A Village in Wiltshire, Edward Brinkworth, a Lacock shopkeeper during the first half of the twentieth century, recalled his childhood days when the canal was in full working order. He said, 'the barges used to come in at the Bell with loads of coal and unload. The barges were about 30 or 40 feet long and drawn by horses. Sometimes two donkeys were used.'

Lacock Wharf today. The Wharf is on the right. The road on the left crosses the course of the canal. The Bell Inn is beyond the bushes hidden from view.

Ray Mill Bridge near Lacock about 1900.

Leaving Lacock the canal runs parallel to the River Avon, past Lackham House and on to Pewsham. It is along this stretch of canal that Bryant would have taken his boat under Naish Hill double bridge. By the 1990s this bridge had all but collapsed, but help was at hand. As part of its restoration programme the Wilts & Berks Canal Trust spent three years working to renovate the bridge. This was successfully completed in May 2009 when the Duchess of Cornwall officiated at the re-opening ceremony.

50   Census returns.

Pewsham

A couple of miles further and Bryant arrived at Pewsham. Here he was faced with a flight of three locks which raised the canal by nearly thirty feet. No doubt at busy times boats queued in both directions to await their turn to enter the locks.

Disaster struck in 1830 when all trade on the canal came to a grinding halt. A boat sank in one of the locks at Pewsham and canal traffic both north and southbound backed up. It took two labourers and probably several days to lift the boat out.[51] Damage to locks was quite a regular occurrence. John Provis of Chippenham was charged ten shillings to repair the lock gates at Melksham, when the master of his boat,

The Duchess of Cornwall re-opening Naish Hill double bridge in 2009.

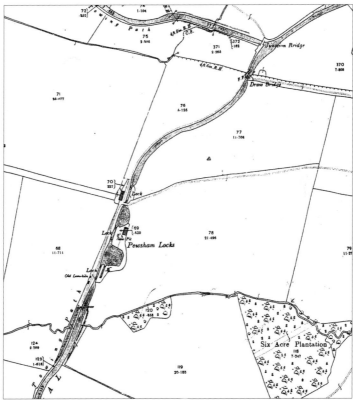

The canal junction and Pewsham locks about 1880. The sawpit and limekiln can be seen. The Lock cottage is next to the top lock.

51 WSA Traders and collectors register.

John Matthews, had smashed into the locks, no doubt once again holding up traffic until they were repaired.

Several industries developed around Pewsham Locks. Beside the canal was a limekiln, the lime and coal to fuel the kiln being brought to Pewsham by canal. Lime was burnt for both agricultural use, to improve acid soil, and for the construction industry in the production of building mortar. No doubt the kiln provided the raw materials for the building of the locks, bridges and lock cottage.

Alongside the locks was a dry dock and large 'basin'. A sawpit was located nearby and carpenters were regularly employed at Pewsham. It is not clear if boats were built at Pewsham. No records have been

(clockwise, from top left) Pewsham top lock about 2007;
Pewsham middle lock undergoing restoration by the Wilts and Berks Canal Trust . The dry dock is in the background;
Remains of the lock cottage showing steps leading to what is thought to be a cellar. The local branch of the Wilts and Berks Canal Trust have been carrying out exploratory excavations;
The sawpit at Pewsham Locks excavated by the Wilts and Berks Canal Trust.

Wilts & Berks Canal Trust work party at Pewsham.

Restoration work on Middle Lock, July 2009.

found to confirm that they were and so the debate continues. It is certain, however, with a dry dock and sawpit available, that Pewsham was used to repair or overhaul boats, especially as the author of 'In Tow' felt it important enough to comment that he saw the remains of section boats at Pewsham.

Beside the top lock of the flight was the Lock Cottage. In the early part of the nineteenth century several lockkeepers were employed at Pewsham, among these Thomas Phillips, Thomas Fulford and William Hiskins, each spending a year or two as lockkeeper before moving on.[52]

By 1816 Mr and Mrs Brown were living at the Lock Cottage. Late one July evening in that year they became victims of a burglary. This was a particularly nasty incident because, after stealing valuables, clothing and private possessions, the thieves threatened to murder both Mr and Mrs Brown in an attempt to 'obtain a greater booty'. They probably thought money was held on behalf of the Canal Company and that the Browns would hand it over when threatened. Mrs Brown managed to escape through a back window of the cottage, but in doing so broke her leg. She crawled away from the cottage and was later found sheltering under a hedge. Mr Brown was eventually released unharmed and the thieves made their getaway. Three days later the gang were apprehended and taken to Calne for 'examination'. They were named as John Slie or Sly 'a notorious gypsey', William Herbert, John Coleman Peer and Harriet Baker.[53]

Sixteen year old Peer turned Queen's evidence and was remanded to Marlborough Gaol. The other three were remanded to Salisbury Gaol for trial which took place on 5th August at Salisbury Assizes. It was reported that Sly and Herbert were both sentenced to death, but were later reprieved.[54] Harriet Baker appeared in court but according to the assize records there was no prosecution, and she was released.[55]

There is no record of how long the Browns remained

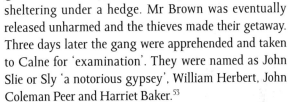

52 WSA Disbursements Ledger.
53 Simpsons Salisbury Gazette July 1816.
54 Salisbury Journal August 1816.
55 England and Wales Criminal Registers.

at Pewsham Lock cottage, but a few years later the Hodgson family had moved in. On the 1841 census, sixty year old R Hodson was described as a Canal Agent. This was Richard Hodgson who, according to the canal records, had been at Pewsham since the 1820s. Ten years later a relation, William Hodgson and his family, had taken over Lock Cottage. William was described as Canal Surveyor and the family remained at Pewsham into the 1880s.

Other members of the Hodgson family had close links with the Wilts & Berks Canal. According to the company's disbursements ledger John Hodgson was regularly employed as a carpenter and mason at Pewsham during the 1850s. In all probability this was William's brother, living at the Lock House in Dauntsey. The family tradition followed into the next generation when William's son, another William, followed in his uncle John's footsteps, being employed by the canal company as a carpenter at Pewsham.

By the early 1890s the Hodgson family had left Pewsham and the Canal Agent at the Lock cottage was James Pratt. Within a few years he too had moved and the cottage was then occupied by Luke Bishop and his wife Alice. The 1895 trade directory lists Bishop as a boat builder, as did the 1901 census. These were the final few years in the life of the canal and in reality Bishop was probably scratching a living repairing boats rather than building new ones.

Following the collapse of the aqueduct in 1901, and the later abandonment of the canal, the locks were left gradually to decay, and the lock cottage was abandoned. With the outbreak of the Second World War the area was used by the military to practice demolition techniques and much of the damage seen at the locks today dates from that period.

A drawbridge on the Wilts and Berks canal. It is possible that this is the drawbridge between Pewsham locks and Chippenham Junction.

Junction Bridge and on to Stanley

Having passed through Pewsham top lock, Bryant with his load of coal continued northwards and within a short distance reached Chippenham Junction. This was the turn for the Chippenham arm of the canal and it is here that he started his final leg of the trip to Chippenham. Today there is no evidence of the junction or the bridge that crossed the canal, the area having been levelled and returned to arable use.

Derry Hill Bridge, looking towards Derry Hill. The two cars on the right of the picture are about to cross the course of the canal. It is thought that this bridge was known as Navvies bridge locally.

Leaving Bryant to travel the Chippenham arm, any boats that were heading towards Wootton Bassett and Swindon would continue on the main line of the canal heading for the turnpike road, now the A4. The canal, on reaching the road, went under Derry Hill Bridge. Today the bridge has been levelled and the busy A4 cuts through the canal course. There is little to show that the bridge ever existed although remnants can still be seen in the undergrowth between the car showroom and Forest Gate. A brown information sign announces to car drivers that they are crossing the canal.

From the A4 the canal continues, in various states of disrepair, through Studley and on to Stanley. It is along this section that the aqueduct crossing the River Marden collapsed in 1901 and effectively ended the life of the canal. A further collapse took place in 1997 and the aqueduct has now all but disappeared.

Immediately after the aqueduct Stanley locks raised the canal by a further seventeen feet. One of the canal characters was the Stanley lockkeeper, Jane Brittain, a widow originally from Lyneham. She was lockkeeper at Stanley for over 20 years and was reportedly still working in 1861 at the age of 74. She died a few years later and local man John Dolman, took over as lockkeeper.

In January 1832 there was a break-in at the Lock House. Like the incident at Pewsham the thieves probably believed that there was company cash held on the premises. Despite handing over some cash to the thieves the Greenman family were threatened with death if they did not hand over more money. The family were roughly treated; Jane Greenman was violently dragged downstairs and threatened with a crowbar. Eventually the robbers, having realised that there was no more money, left the cottage and made their getaway. They were apprehended a few days later in Devizes. The prisoners, William Isaac, Joseph George and Robert Star stood trial at the Lent Assizes of 1832 and, having been found guilty, were all sentenced to death. This was later commuted to transportation for life.[56]

James Hood, a boat owner and trader during the early part of the nineteenth century, traded from Stanley Locks. He was a general carrier and the canal company ledgers show that he carried all manner of goods, ranging from wheat, corn and oats to timber, bricks and stone. He regularly collected potatoes from Stanley Wharf for delivery around the district.[57] Also at Stanley was the boat builder and carpenter Matthew Fawkes, who according to the canal company ledgers was regularly employed during the second decade of the nineteenth century repairing boats and locks.[58]

Stanley Bridge Farm. The farmhouse was probably originally one of the wharf buildings. It is thought that there was stabling at the rear. Salt was stored in the farmhouse. The yard to the front of the farmhouse was the wharf.

The wharf at Stanley was next to the Navigation Bridge and is today known as Stanley Bridge Farm. The remains of the canal lay in front of the farmhouse and the yard is the site of the wharf. The current owners confirm the postal address is still 'The Wharf'. Stanley Wharf must have been busy as it boasted its own wharfinger or wharf manager. During the 1850s the wharfinger was David Bull who probably had known and laboured at the Wharf all his life. Bull was the

56 Wiltshire Gazette March 1832.
57 WSA 2424/36: Toll ledgers.
58 WSA 2424/31: Ledger.

son of the local coal merchant, and it is not difficult to imagine that as a young man he collected coal from the wharf.

Bull lived close to the wharf, and according to the census records his neighbour was William Whitworth. This was the same Whitworth who forty years earlier had been responsible for building the Wilts & Berks canal.

In 1851 Whitworth, a widower, who had lived in Stanley for a number of years, had retired from building canals and in the census was described as a 'proprietor of land and coal works'. He owned an estate in Kington St Michael and was also a major shareholder in the Forest of Dean Coal Works Company.

His death, at home aged 84, was announced in the Devizes and Wiltshire Gazette of 12 February 1857 and he is buried at Bremhill church, just up the hill from where he lived.

William Whitworth's tomb in Bremhill Churchyard.

From Stanley the Wilts & Berks Canal continued for a further forty-one miles, to join the Thames at Abingdon, but for this book it is at Stanley the journey along the main line of the canal ends.

From Semington, where James Bryant joined the canal and registered his cargo and obtained his permit, to Stanley is only eleven miles. From Lacock to Stanley is a mere five, but they were important miles to Chippenham and the surrounding area during the nineteenth century.

8. The Chippenham Branch

Having turned on to the Chippenham branch or arm James Bryant now started the final part of his journey to Chippenham. The branch followed the natural contours, avoiding the need for any locks on its two miles into Chippenham. Today much of the canal has been lost, either to agriculture or housing, but during the eighteen seventies and eighties when Bryant regularly navigated the canal the branch was still busy and supported agriculture and industry along its banks.

Forest Brickworks

Within a short distance of Chippenham Junction, and adjacent to the canal, was Forest Brickworks. Its location was intentional as William Whitworth, the canal engineer, decided that Pewsham would be an ideal location to manufacture bricks for the new canal. The canal records show that James Heath was making bricks at Pewsham during the late 1790s;[59] the brickyard supplied the thousands of bricks needed to build Stanley aqueduct.

By the early nineteenth century John Cullis was producing bricks at Forest brickworks. Pigot's 1842 Commercial Directory lists Cullis as a brickmaker living in Cook Street. Several other members of the Cullis family were also living in Chippenham and Pewsham at this time, all brickmakers and no doubt linked to the family business. In the early years of the century the brickyard proved to be successful. The canal records show Cullis's bricks being shipped around the district with many destined for Lacock and Melksham. The Canal Company was a major customer. In 1821 Cullis supplied bricks to the value of £100 for repairs to the canal,[60] and he continued to supply them for the next thirty years. In 1849 a major consignment was purchased for the sum of £38.

As trade was brisk Cullis decided to expand his business. During the 1830s he diversified into boat building. He paid the canal

---

59   WSA 2424: Ledgers
60   WSA 2424/ 28 to 32

Jays Bridge, mid-1960s. It is at this point that Forest Lane crossed the road.

company two pounds per year for a, 'Wet Dock on the eastern bank of the canal at the brickyard on the Rooks Nest Farm on the Chippenham branch for the purpose of building boats'.[61]

John Cullis finally retired from the business during the 1850s; he was by then in his seventies. Although it is unclear who took over the business, it seems likely that William Cullis, probably John's son, continued producing bricks at Pewsham Forest.

The Cullis family fortunes then took a turn for the worse. In 1853 William Cullis was declared insolvent. In his examination he was described as a brickmaker and licensed victualler of River Street, Chippenham. William was not uncommon in having two trades. Brick-making was a seasonal occupation where the clay was dug during spring and summer and left to be 'prepared' by the frosts of winter.[62] Several other members of the Cullis family also suffered from the decline in the business, because over the following years a number of them, all brickmakers, left the Chippenham area in search of work. It is likely that the breakdown of the Cullis family business was closely linked to the failing fortunes of the Canal Company. As maintenance on the canal declined so the demand for bricks tailed off.

There is no record of when the Cullis family finally left the brickyard, but by the 1870s the Canal Company ledgers show that Brinkworth of Chippenham was regularly transporting bricks and pipes from Pewsham Forest to his yard at the wharf. James Bryant, who of course worked for Brinkworth, regularly carried bricks from Pewsham to Melksham and Lacock. It is likely that Brinkworth had taken ownership of the brickworks, especially as his advertisements of the 1870s and 1880s described him as a coal merchant and brick manufacturer.

Rooks Nest and Deep Cutting

Having passed the brickworks the route of the canal follows the southern boundary of what is today Pewsham housing estate.

---

61 WSA 2424/9: Traders register
62 British Brick Society Information 40

This is thought to be Deep Cutting bridge towards the end of the nineteenth century.

Within a short distance Bryant would have reached the first bridge on the Chippenham branch. This was Jays Bridge, which carried Forest Lane over the canal. Today there is no sign of the bridge apart from a slight rise in the lane before it drops towards Pewsham Way, but some local residents believe that the bridge still exists, buried under the lane.

Nearby is Rooks Nest Farm. The toll registers record deliveries of timber and hurdles to 'Rooks Nest'; however there is no record of a wharf at Rooks Nest so boats would have unloaded straight on to the canal bank.

The remains of Deep Cutting bridge in the early 1990s. The Canal course was cleared at the time Pewsham Estate was built. The area is now again covered by vegetation

Travelling on toward Chippenham the route of the canal crosses Canal Road and enters a deep cutting. Although heavily overgrown, the route of the canal can be seen quite easily. Within the undergrowth are the remains of Deep Cutting Bridge. Both Jays Bridge and Deep Cutting Bridge appear on the Ordnance Survey map of 1940, but it is thought by local residents that Deep Cutting Bridge was used for military exercises during the Second World War, which led to its demolition. However when in 1965 Wiltshire County Council published a notice diverting a footpath in Pewsham, it included the following description:

> Length of Footpath No. 14 Pewsham, leading from C.R.B.12 to the
> south of Jay's Bridge in a general westerly direction up to and over
> Deep Cutting Bridge over the old Wilts & Berks Canal at its junction

with Footpath No.29, a distance of approximately 590 yards shall be stopped up.[63]

This of course suggests that Deep Cutting Bridge and probably Jay's Bridge were still in situ as late as 1965.

Englands

Painting of Englands Bridge by J.H. Jolliffe dated 1866. The cottages in the background are in Wood Lane.

The canal continued through Deep Cutting and emerged on what is now Pewsham Way near the lane leading to the sewage works. From this point Pewsham Way follows the course of the old canal. This was part of Borough Lands and the canal cut through the area known as Great and Little Englands. Close to the Webbington Road roundabout is the site of the final bridge on the Chippenham arm, known as Englands Bridge. It was in 1912 that the Town Council asked the Canal Company for permission to demolish Englands Bridge, because it was in such a poor state of repair.

Children from Wood Lane would often walk across the footpaths in Englands to play around the canal and the bridge. It was near Englands Bridge that, in July 1898, an awful accident occurred. Five-year-old William Hatherall, son of Will Hatherall a local labourer, was playing with his sister Jenny and some other children on the banks of the canal, when he suddenly slipped and fell in. The children tried to save him but couldn't reach, so in a panic ran home to raise the alarm.

Perkins map of 1904 Showing the canal crossing Borough Lands.

Ambrose Neate, a twelve year old boy from Wood Lane was walking nearby when he heard from one of the children that the boy had fallen into the canal. He ran to the canal bank, and jumped in to save the little lad. Unfortunately the canal was particularly overgrown with weeds and all that could be seen was William's hat. Ambrose continued searching the water for a quarter of an hour and eventually found the boy, but, despite his best efforts, William Hatherall was dead.

---

63   London Gazette 1965

William was buried in London Road Cemetery on the 29 July. The inquest was held at the Three Crowns Inn a few days later, where a verdict of accidental death by drowning was recorded. The Coroner, W E M Brown, thought that Ambrose Neate should be commended for his bravery. In response a subscription was started by Mr J (Joe) Buckle, Secretary of the Chippenham Swimming Club, and with the contributions a silver watch and chain were presented to Ambrose by the Mayor, Mr L H Marshall.[64]

This was not an isolated incident – along the length of the canal there were frequent tragedies. In 1844 George Dedman and Mary Ann Hull were playing on an empty canal boat moored in Chippenham. As the boat rocked in the water the children lost their footing and fell in. The two five year olds could not be saved.[65]

Sometimes there was a happier ending. The Devizes and Wiltshire Gazette in 1835 reported that a young boy fell into the canal near Chippenham, again while playing on the empty coal boats. He was lucky. Henry Edgecombe of Chippenham was passing by, saw him fall in and managed to save him. The same newspaper in 1826 reported a mystery. The body of an unknown man had been found in the canal near the bridge at Pewsham, probably at the junction with the Chippenham branch. His hat and stick were found on the towpath but when he was pulled out of the canal his pockets were found to be empty. Who was he? More importantly had he jumped in or had he been pushed? These questions were never answered and at the inquest he remained unidentified and the verdict of the jury was quite simply 'Found drowned'.

(top) Newspaper headline from the Bath Herald of August 1898 reporting on the presentation of of the silver watch to Ambrose Neate in recognition of his bravery in trying to save the drowning boy; (above) Picture of Ambrose Neate as it appeared in the the People newspaper, 7 August 1898.

Chippenham Tunnel

Continuing along the Arm beyond Englands Bridge was Chippenham tunnel. This was the tunnel that was the subject of the dispute between the town and Canal Company in 1800. The first view that boat crews had was the fine stone portal.[66] No doubt in 1803, when the tunnel was built, the portal was designed to impress visiting boat crews and acknowledge the status of the town. By contrast the mouth at the other end of the tunnel was rather plain and made of brick;

Joe Buckle, Secretary of Chippenham Swimming Club;

64   Chippenham Museum and Heritage Centre: Buckle scrapbooks
65   Hampshire Advertiser and Salisbury Guardian July 1844, Inquest report.
66   www.gentle-highway.info Simon Nuttall's article on Chippenham Tunnel

Ordnance Survey map of 1886 Chippenham. The Wharf is top centre, the tunnel at the centre of the map.

it did not really need to make a statement when the boats were leaving town.

After emerging from the ninety-yard tunnel, it was then a short distance to the Wharf. The canal reappeared in what is today the car park opposite the police station, and continued behind Westmead School. It is said that the schoolchildren would climb the wall behind the school to watch the horses towing the boats between the tunnel and wharf. As the towpath did not go through the tunnel, the horses had to be unhitched and led over the tunnel, the boat being legged through.

There is an ambiguity along this stretch of canal. How were boats turned round to return along the Chippenham arm? It is quite clear that the stretch from the wharf to the tunnel was narrow, and where it did widen slightly was probably used to moor boats. It certainly was not wide enough to turn a boat that could be up to seventy foot long. So it is quite clear that boats departing needed to be towed backwards through the tunnel. Beyond the tunnel one would expect to find a turning point in the canal, known as a winding hole. Early maps and canal records do not mention a winding hole and not until 1817 do the Town Council records show the canal company applied for 'leave to cut a part of the land at England's adjoining the Canal for making a place to turn the boats.' So are we led to believe that boats travelled backwards along the two mile Chippenham Arm for the first seventeen years of its life?

9. Chippenham

Chippenham Wharf in Timber Street was the final destination on the Chippenham Arm. At its peak over nine thousand tons of coal were landed here each year. Timber Street was a busy commercial area with several coal merchants surrounding the wharf. During the 1830s the commercial directories lists both Charles Hannum and William Rugg selling coal in Timber Street, while John Robbins employed three men in his thriving coal business during the 1840s.

John Provis, a well known Chippenham resident, was listed in Pigot's Commercial Directory of 1822 as a coal and timber merchant with premises in New Road. Not only was Provis trading in the town but he was also involved in boat building, and owned at least one boat which regularly visited the wharf. Not surprisingly his boat brought coal, logs and timber to Chippenham.

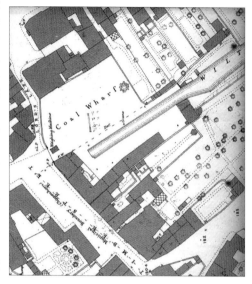

Ordnance Survey map showing Chippenham Wharf and canal during the 1880s

Brinkworth

By the 1860s James Brinkworth had established his coal yard at the wharf. The Brinkworth business was clearly successful as he employed 17 men and 9 boys. The 1861 census described Brinkworth as a coal and slate merchant who had also diversified into brick and drainage pipe manufacturing. The company also owned a number of coal-carrying boats.

View of the Entrance to the Wharf from the Market Place. The building in the centre of the picture is the wharf office. This photo was taken in 1897. The crowds are celebrating the Diamond Jubilee.

Chippenham Wharf offices from Timber Street. To the left of the of the Wharf office can be seen one of the gates to the wharf. The house to the right was The Wharf House.

The Ellen, the Margaret and Flora were all part of James Brinkworth's fleet. Brinkworth's sons, George and Tom, were both employed in the offices in Timber Street, but it was William (W H Brinkworth), the eldest son, who eventually took over the business from his father during the 1870s. At this time William Sidnell[67] of Back Lane was employed as the clerk at the coal wharf offices.

Returning to James Bryant on his journey from Camerton, the wharf was the final destination for his boatload of coal. Arriving at the wharf he would find Daniel Dorsett waiting to help unload the boat. Dorsett, possibly a relative of Bryant's mate Thomas Dorset,[68] was employed as a labourer at the wharf and his instructions would be to get the boat unloaded as quickly as possible. The orders and byelaws of the canal company stated that 'a boat should be discharged of its lading with all convenient speed and to leave the wharf within one hour'. The penalty for failing to comply with these regulations was a hefty forty shillings.

Once unloaded William Bluitt and William Wooton, both employed as wharf carters, probably took responsibility for delivering the coal around the town.

Just around the corner from the wharf, in Wood Lane, lived Joseph Matthews, another Chippenham boat owner during the second half of the nineteenth century. Described as a canal trader, he was a general carrier who brought locally grown crops, such as potatoes, grain and barley to the town and supplied the building trade with bricks, timber and stone. Although it is uncertain, there is a suggestion that he may have unloaded his boats in Wood Lane close to the tunnel.

Most of the Chippenham boatmen lived within a short distance of the wharf. The census returns during the nineteenth century indicate that both Wood Lane and Blind Lane were centres of the boating fraternity.

James Brinkworth ,the founder of Coal Merchants business at the wharf.

The Wharf

What did the Chippenham wharf look like? It was an area of 2 roods 9½ poles, just over half an acre, adjoining the Market Place, described as 'being the centre of town, level with a good

---

67   1871 Census Returns
68   1861 to 1881 Census Returns

Chippenham Wharf about 1895. The house in the background is 15 Timber Street, known as The Wharf House. The man rowing the boat is William Brinkworth and it is thought the girls in the boat with him are Mabel Freeth (left) and her sister Lilien. The lady stood at the gate is probably their mother Ellen. The Freeth family were living at The Wharf House at the time the photo was taken. It is thought that Mr Freeth was a corn merchant.

approach'.[69] There were several buildings that formed the wharf premises. The Wharf House fronted Timber Street and by the end of the nineteenth century was known as no 15 Timber Street. It was a substantial four bedroomed residence, with cellars, kitchens and a loft probably originally built with the Wharfinger in mind. Adjacent to the Wharf House was the general office, which included the store rooms and a ten ton weighbridge by Bartlett and Son of Bristol. The building had distinctive round windows on the upper floor. To the rear there were various stores and stabling within the wharf yard.

William Brinkworth continued his business selling coal and building materials from the wharf until 1914. This was, of course, long after the canal became derelict following the collapse of Stanley aqueduct in 1901. The wharf became little more than a storage yard and, ironically, most of the coal and building materials sold were brought to the town by rail.

In 1915 the wharf was sold at auction and R E Rudman, the Chippenham builder, used it as his yard. Some years later, around the Second World War, the wharf was turned over to road transport and became the town bus station.

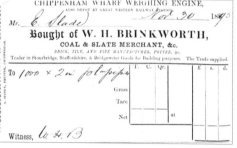

Mr Slade had ordered 1000 two inch clay pipes from Brinkworth's yard. Brinkworth had a second yard close to the railway Station in Chippenham.

69 Chippenham Museum and Heritage Centre: Auction catalogue 1915

Life, Death and Leisure

But the canal was not all hard work and industry. There was a lighter side to life by the canal. Arnold Platts, in his book, A History Of Chippenham AD853 to 1946 says that many residents remembered pleasure trips along the canal, when groups of children would be taken as far as Pewsham locks. No doubt there was great excitement as the boat went though the tunnel.

Chippenham wharf seen from the air early 1920s. The distinctive double roof of the The Wharf House can be seen at the centre of the photo. The canal has been filled in but the sheds and stabling for 8 horses can be seen behind the Wharf House. In the centre of the yard the two ton crane used to unload boats is still in place.

It was not only the children that enjoyed days out on the canal. John Trow would take groups from the local chapels for canal outings on his boat the Helen.[70] They would leave the wharf and travel the Chippenham arm enjoying the scenery and wildlife. Perhaps Trow would moor up and allow his passengers to walk beside the canal. Joliffe's painting of 1866 shows an idyllic picture of a family strolling along the towpath in Englands.

Did the young men go fishing in the canal? Did they swim in the canal in the summer to cool off? Doubtless they did, although officially this was forbidden. The Canal Company rule book said:

70   J A Chamberlain, Chippenham

John Trow on his boat at Chippenham wharf. Standing behind him is William Brinkworth. Trow would regularly take chapel parties for pleasure cruises along the canal. It was always thought this boat was called Helen, but it has recently been confirmed the boat was in fact called "Faith".

That if any person should wilfully throw in any carrion or other nuisance or shall bathe in any part of this Canal or shall angle or fish with nets or otherwise without being entitled to do so by the Act for making the said Canal every such person shall forfeit and pay any sum not exceeding Five Pounds.

The rules were enforced across the district and amongst the reported cases three young men appeared at the Police Court in Swindon charged with fishing in the Wilts & Berks canal.[71] They were found guilty and fined £1 each. However, if you had permission and a licence the fishing was reported as first rate and the canal was noted for its fine tench.[72]

Winters of one hundred years ago must have been much colder than today. The records show that the canal froze regularly and 'ice breakers' were employed by the canal company. The ice on the canal must have been pretty thick as Arnold Platts also tells us that many people recalled skating on the frozen canal in the town. Edward Brinkworth, the shopkeeper of Lacock, remembered as a boy in the late nineteenth century skating as far as Chippenham Wharf when the canal had frozen over.

71   Bristol Mercury June 1879
72   Fishing Gazette 1890

The Rose and Crown about 1880. Many of the workers of the canal frequented the Rose and Crown and for a short time it was renamed as the Barge Inn.

Where did the canal workers and boatmen spend what little leisure time they had? The Rose and Crown in the Causeway was for a short time also known as the Barge Inn[73] and was a regular meeting place for the boating community of Chippenham.

Finally there was an unusual request to use a canal boat as a hearse. In 1841 William Dunsford, the Wilts & Berks Manager of the time, wrote his will. He specified that he should be buried in Chippenham Cemetery, of which he was a part owner. He stipulated that his coffin should be transported to Chippenham, on the 'Sabbeth day', by canal boat, accompanied by his 'faithful clerk' and sons. Dunsford died some years later and was buried in Swindon!

The corner of Timber Street and Wood Lane towards the end of the nineteenth century. This is the area that most of the Chippenham canal folk lived.

73   Chippenham Museum and Heritage Centre

10. Canal Boat Registration

The Canal Boat Acts of 1877 and 1884 introduced the requirement for registration of boats across the canal network. Registration of canal boats was established to improve the accommodation standards of those who lived on board and to ensure that canal children attended school.

As trade on the canals started to decline, mainly due to the increasing competition from the railways, so boatmen increasingly suffered financial hardship. Many responded by giving up the family home and moving their families on to the boat. With the family on board there was an additional financial saving. With his wife available to work on the boat, the boatman no longer had a need to employ a mate. The children could also help by looking after and leading the horse, usually at the expense of attending school.

This trend spread across the country and Chippenham was no exception. The thirty-ton boat Queen, which originated in Chippenham, regularly journeyed between Bristol, Bath and Chippenham. Thomas Sheppard and his wife Maria crewed the boat.[74] Even after their daughter Rhoda was born in 1878 the family continued to live on board travelling the canal. In fact many families were raised and babies born on canal boats. In 1881 Elizabeth Bryant of Melksham told the census enumerator she was born on the boat Ellen.

Living on board was cramped. Accommodation took up valuable carrying capacity and therefore the boatman kept the living

Breakfast in the Cuddy. From The Quiver - *An illustrated magazine of 1897. This picture clearly shows how cramped the living space on board the boats was.*

---

74   1881 Census return. On Census night the the Queen was moored at Bristol.

A boatman's stove from the Wilts and Berks Canal Trust collection.

quarters to an absolute minimum. There were many examples where families of six or more were living, cooking and sleeping in a cabin no bigger than seven by nine feet. As a result, diseases such as smallpox and cholera would spread quickly through the boating community. As the victims were constantly on the move it was difficult to contain the infection. There were reports in some areas of boats leaving a trail of sickness and disease.[75]

Acts of Parliament introduced minimum standards on boats. Inevitably this meant larger cabins with a corresponding decrease in the amount of cargo that could be carried. This reduced the earnings of the boatmen and therefore registration became hugely unpopular, with registration evasion becoming widespread.

On the southern stretch of the Wilts & Berks canal both Chippenham and Calne were designated Registration Authorities. In Chippenham this meant that the Local Sanitary Board was responsible for registering boats, ensuring they met the standards required by the 1877 Act of Parliament. Once registered the boat owner was obliged to display the registration number and place of registration on the side of his boat. Chippenham District Local Board took its responsibilities seriously and at its meeting of 20 August 1878 the Clerk said that he had received instruction on registration of boats and agreed that a notice should be issued to canal boat traders. The 1877 Act however was not effective as it lacked the power to check up on compliance.

The 1884 Act was introduced requiring local boards to appoint an inspector and to provide an annual report detailing action they had taken supervising canal boat registration and ensuring children from canal boats attended school. The canal inspectors were authorised to enter boats to ensure that they were complying with their registration certificates. This meant with the introduction of the 1884 Act that there were two distinct duties placed on the Local Boards. First, the requirement to register boats and assess the living accommodation, and second, the ongoing inspection of boats and related reports.

Chippenham Urban Sanitary Board took responsibility for canal boat registration, and John Lightfoot, who already held the position of Town Surveyor, was appointed Surveyor of Boats in July 1885.

Extract from the Chippenham Local Board minutes of August 1878. Introducing the 1877 Canal Boats Act to the Council.

75   Hansard: Report from the select Committee on the Canal Boats Act (1877) Amendment Bill

The inspection of boats fell to Chippenham Rural Sanitary Authority, the District Council of its day. In July 1885 William Tanner of Lacock Wharf was appointed Inspector of Boats. At that time twenty to thirty boats passed along the canal each week and Tanner was given authority to detain and inspect any boats where he thought there was a contravention of the Act.

The Chippenham registration and inspection records have been lost but it is thought that the following boats were among those registered at Chippenham.

Annie	Owner	Joseph Kilminster or Kilmister
Bertha	Owner	Not known
Queen	Master	Thomas Sheppard
Victory	Owner	George Hudd
Ellen	Owner	Brinkworth
Flora	Owner	Brinkworth
Margaret	Owner	Brinkworth
Endeavour	Owner	Not known

(Endeavour may have been registered elsewhere but originated from Lacock)

The Chippenham boards must have carried out their duties diligently. In 1898 the Local Government Board carried out a check of the inspection reports and found them to be satisfactory.[76] Despite the diligence of the boards, they could not hide the fact that canal trade had all but ceased. In September 1901 the Clerk to the Chippenham Rural District Council wrote to the Local Government Board asking for permission to withdraw the appointment of canal boat inspector on the grounds that there were no boats passing through the District. The Local Government Board wrote back agreeing to the request, and accordingly Mr Lewis, the Inspector at the time, was made redundant.[77]

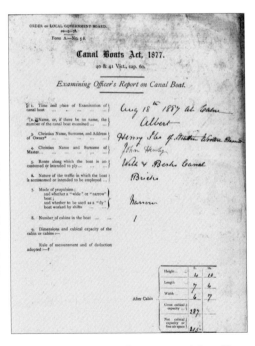

Extract from an Examining officers report from Calne. Dated 1887. The report is for a boat called Albert

76   WSA G3/100/6: Chippenham RDC Minute Book
77   WSA G3/100/7: Chippenham RDC Minute Book

11. The Canal Today

Part of the derelict Chippenham Arm in the undergrowth close to Pewsham Way.

Today the old canal regularly makes the headlines, as the Wilts & Berks Canal Trust continues in its project to restore it. The aim is once again to see boats travel from the Kennet & Avon to the Thames at Abingdon and I have no doubt that, with the enthusiasm and commitment of the Trust, their dream will become a reality. Locally, there is a proposal that the area around Pewsham lock could be developed into a historic centre.

I am not so sure about the Chippenham arm, much of which is now part of a housing estate or under a busy road and lies largely forgotten. I think that, to restore it would be a mammoth undertaking, so it is likely that the arm will remain hidden. But the signs of the canal are still there and, with a bit of exploration, much of the route along the perimeter of Pewsham Estate can still be traced. I also think of the tunnel each time I travel along Pewsham Way and Avenue La Fleche. Is it still there hidden in the undergrowth next to the roundabout waiting to be rediscovered? I like to think so and maybe, just maybe, one day somebody will look for it.

The canal is remembered on Pewsham Estate by some of the street names. Do many residents of Whitworth Road realise their namesake was such a significant part of the canal's history?

But it is at the bus station in Timber Street that the canal in Chippenham is recalled. Chippenham Civic Society erected a blue plaque to mark the site of the wharf from over a hundred years ago. For a short time in November 2006 the wharf reappeared. Workmen redeveloping the bus station uncovered the remains of the canal terminus. Before it was covered over again archaeologists were able to examine the area and recover objects from the canal objects that many people in the town can say were used by their forefathers.

It is at this point that this book closes, but the story is not complete. There is still more to be discovered about the canal and those who lived by it. What happened to the hero Ambrose Neate? What happened to the baby Rhoda who lived on the boat Queen with her parents? Is the tunnel mouth still there, just covered in vegetation? If having read this book you are able to fill any gaps please let the Curator at Chippenham Museum and Heritage Centre know.

The Chippenham Civic Society blue plaque, that remembers the canal in the town.

Last glimpse of canal

(above) Chippenham bus station in 2008. The small inset picture of the wharf shows the same location. The Wharf House and buildings to the left have been demolished. The wall to the left of the modern picture is probably the back wall of the wharf store.

(right) Newspaper cutting from the Chippenham Gazette and Herald of 9 November 2006 reporting the uncovering of the canal terminus in Timber Street.

(below left) Excavation during the bus station development
(below right) As this book goes to print in 2011 the stretch of canal below Pewsham locks has once again been returned to water.

Appendix 1
List of Boatmen and other Canal Workers from the Chippenham area

William Bluitt Born about 1850 Employed as a carter at the coal wharf. Lived in Blind Lane, Chippenham.

William Boucher Boucher was born in Lacock. On census night 1881 he was moored at Raby Wharf, Bathampton. He was the boatman in charge on the boat *Harriet*.

James Bryant Born Chippenham 1825. Master on W H Brinkworth's boat.

Thomas Bunner Born Chippenham about 1804, described as a canal carrier. During the 1820s to 1840s lived in Studley, later moved to King Street, Melksham. Thomas's sons Alfred and Thomas also became canal carriers.

John Clark Born Chippenham 1831. Master of the coal barge *Ellen*. The *Ellen* was owned by James Brinkworth.

Frank Cole In 1881 Cole was a barge boy on the *Emma* moored at Regent Street Wharf, Swindon. The census stated he was born in Lacock.

James Curtis Born in Chippenham, sixty-one year old Curtis was the master of the boat *Fanny*. In March 1871 he was moored at St Stephens, Bristol.

Robert Downing Born Chippenham 1817. 1851 Census lists him as a boat master living in Melksham.

George Earl Little is known about George Earl. He died in the Chippenham Workhouse in 1880 aged 63 The Chippenham cemetery records describe him as a boatman.

John Franklin Listed in the 1841 census as a boatman living in Wood Lane, later moved to Westmead Lane.

Thomas Fulford Thought to have been the Chippenham wharfinger in the early years of the nineteenth century.

Maria Gregory Born Chippenham in 1857. Married Thomas Sheppard in 1876 and lived on board the *Queen*.

Edwin Haines On the 1861 census fourteen year old, Chippenham born, Haines was the mate on the *Flora* moored at Melksham.

Charles Hannum Thought to have been the Chippenham wharfinger during the 1830s, declared bankrupt in 1833.

James Harding Listed in the 1841 census a boatman living in Wood Lane.

James Hiskins Hiskins appeared at the Bath police court in January 1891 for contravening the Canal Boat Acts. The report of the hearing said he was the owner of the boat *Charity*, and came from Chippenham. William Taylor, the master of the boat also appeared in the court for similar offences.

Joseph Kilminster In August 1890 Kilminster or Kilmister applied to the Chippenham Board to register his boat the *Annie*, previously known as *Himilaya*. By 1891 he and his wife Annamarie owned the boat *Ready Penny* and on census night they were moored at Pewsham.

Joseph Matthews Snr Mathews lived in Wood Lane and was variously described as a boatman and barge owner.

Joseph Matthews Jnr Son of Joseph Snr, born about 1830. Expanded the business and owned several boats employing amongst others G Brittain, W Sheppard and James Silk. He was described in the census as a canal trader.

James Matthews Probably a relation of the Joseph Matthews. The 1841 census listed him as a boatman living in Wood Lane.

John Morrell Born in Chippenham about 1853, lived in Wood Lane and worked on a coal boat.

George Neate Born in Slaughterford about 1876. He was the wharfinger at Chippenham in the early 1890s. Lived in Timber Street.

Jacob Powell Mate on the boat *Endeavour*, born in Chippenham about 1840.

Thomas Sheppard Master of Chippenham registered boat *Queen*.

James Silk Snr Born 1827 in Calne, worked as a steerer or master for Joseph Matthews Jnr of Chippenham. In early 1881 Silk and his son Robert were working the boat *Express*.

Robert Silk Thought to be the son of James Silk Snr. Worked with his father on the boat *Express*.

James Silk Jnr Son of James Snr worked as a steerer or master for Joseph Matthews Jnr during the late 1870s. Born in Calne, the census of 1871 described him as a 15 year old boat boy.

William Slade Twenty-two year old Slade was shown in the 1861 census as foreman at the coal wharf.

William Taylor Master of the boat *Charity*. The boat was owned by James Hiskins of Chippenham. January 1891 both Taylor and Hiskins appeared at the Bath police court for contravening the Canal Boat Acts.

Townsend Possibly *William Townsend*, steerer for John Provis of Chippenham. The *Devizes and Wiltshire Gazette* of 18 February 1835 reported that Townsend, a bargeman from Chippenham whilst returning with his boat from Bristol fell into the canal and drowned.

John Trow John Trow is seen in the photograph of Chippenham Wharf.[78] Trow is at the tiller in the photograph. Although the

---

78   *A Chippenham Collection* (page 75) published Chippenham Civic Society 1987

boat in the photograph is recorded as the *Helen*, it has now been established that it was called *Faith*. Trow lived in Blind Lane, Chippenham and was well known for taking local groups for pleasure trips on his boat. He died in 1911 aged 84 and is buried in Chippenham cemetery.

Mr Wharry Listed as the Chippenham wharfinger about 1814.

Stephen Wheeler In 1851 lived with his parents in a cottage next to Stanley Bridge Farm, Stanley. Described in the census as a boatman.

John Wilkins Wilkins lived in Wood Lane. He died in 1855 aged 39. The Chippenham cemetery records describe him as a boatman.

William Wooton In 1881 Wootton was employed as a carter at the coal wharf. He lived in Blind Lane.

Appendix Two
List of Subscribers to the Wilts & Berks Canal from Chippenham and surrounding area

Extracted from the Subscribers ledgers of the late Eighteenth and early Nineteenth Century.

John Awdry	Notton
Thomas Brown,	
Executor Ann Brown	Chippenham
William Belcher	Christian Malford
Thomas Bourne	Melksham
Maurice Bissett	Stanton
William Cambridge	Chippenham
Ralph Hale Gaby	Chippenham
Henry Heath	Broad Somerford (Great Somerford)
Matthew Humphries	Chippenham
John Harding	Chippenham

John Heath	Chippenham
Stephen King	Chippenham
Marquis of Lansdown	Bowood
Henry Merewether	Calne
James Montague	Lackham
Earl of Peterborough	Dauntsey
John Pullen	Lyneham
James Pullen	Lyneham
Thomas Pike	Somerford
Revd Dr Pollock	Grittleton
Jasper Rumbold	Lyneham
William Stephens	Chippenham
William Tayler	Chippenham
Stephen Nesey	Melksham
James Tayler	Yatton Keynell
John Moore	Corsham
John Noyes (jnr)	Chippenham
Edgar Frances Austen	Calne
William Whitworth	Burnley, later Stanley
William Knight	Langley Burrell
William Tarrant	Chippenham
Henry Maundrell	Blacklands

Bibliography

Berry W, *Kennet and Avon Navigation*, The History Press 2009

Corfield M.C., *A Guide to the Industrial Archaeology of Wiltshire*, Wiltshire County Council 1978

Chamberlain J A, *Chippenham, Some Notes on its History*, Chippenham Charter Trustees. 1976

Clifford D, *I.K. Brunel. The Construction of the Great Western Railway*, Finial Publishing, 2006

Dalby L.J., *The Wilts and Berks Canal*, Oakwood 2000

Goldney F H, *Records of Chippenham*, Goldney 1889

Hadfield C, *Canals of South and South East England*, David & Charles 1969

Heath F R, *Wiltshire*, Methuen (Little Guides Series) 1913

Jefferies S, *A Chippenham Collection*, Chippenham Civic Society 1987

Lawton B, *Building the Wilts and Berks Canal 1793-1810*, Newcomen

Society 2006

Murray P, *A Village in Wiltshire*, PMA Lacock 1975

Perkins J, *A History of the Borough of Chippenham*, Chippenham 1905

Phillips J, *A General History of Inland Navigation*, C and R Baldwin 1792

Platts A, *A History of Chippenham AD 853 to 1946*, Platts 1946

Priestley J, *Priestley's Navigable Rivers and Canals*, David & Charles, 1969 (facsimile reprint of 1831)

Small D, *Images of England. The Wilts and Berks Canal*, Tempus 2003

Small D, *Wilts and Berks Canal Revisited*, The History Press 2010

Smith C, *Chippenham Walkabout*, Chippenham Civic Society 1977

Stanier P, *Wiltshire in the Age of Steam*, Halsgrove 2006

Stone M, *Chippenham Living Memories of your Town.*, Black Horse 2002

Stone M, *Images Of England. Chippenham*, Tempus 2003

Waylen J, *A History Military and Municipal of the Ancient Borough of the Devizes*, Longman, Brown, & Co 1859

Wilson A, *Forgotten Harvest*, Wilson 1995

Yorke S, *English Canals Explained*, Countryside 2003

Minutes Of Evidence. Canal Boats Act 1877, Amendment Bill, Hansard 1884

Wilts & Berks Account Books, Toll Registers And Disbursement Ledgers, Wiltshire and Swindon Record Office-Series 2424

Chippenham Town Council Minute Books, Chippenham Bailiff Books, Chippenham Borough Minutes 1785 to 1971, Chippenham Museum and Heritage Centre

, ,